R.E.S.C.U. E.:

A Church Navigational System for Transformation

Don't Let Your Church Sink into the Ecclesiastical Graveyard

J. Lindsay Sadler Jr., DMin

CROSSBOOKS

CrossBooks™
A Division of LifeWay
One LifeWay Plaza
Nashville, TN 37234
www.crossbooks.com
Phone: 1-866-768-9010

Scripture quotations taken from the New American Standard Bible®,
Copyright © 1960, 1962, 1963, 1968, 1971, 1972, 1973, 1975, 1977, 1995 by
The Lockman Foundation. Used by permission." (www.Lockman.org)

First published by CrossBooks 08/04/2014

ISBN: 978-1-4627-5191-4 (sc)
ISBN: 978-1-4627-5192-1 (hc)
ISBN: 978-1-4627-5190-7 (e)

Library of Congress Control Number: 2014913494

Printed in the United States of America.

This book is printed on acid-free paper.

CONTENTS

Acknowledgements vii

Preface... ix

Introduction.. xiii

Chapter 1 **R.** – Relationships:..1
Reconciliation/restoration are the keys to
rebuilding relationships. Is there someone in
my fellowship whom I need to forgive, to show
grace, or to love more deeply?

Chapter 2 **E.** – Evaluation and Expectations:.....................21
Evaluation: What truly is the reality of my church?
Expectations of Staff and Members:
Staff: Called or hired? Members: Ministers or
Pew voters?

Chapter 3 **S.** – Streamlined Governance: Who
leads the church?...66

Chapter 4 **C.** – Clear and Concise Vision and Mission:.....92
They are directional markers for the church.
Has the leadership provided a clear direction
for the church?

Chapter 5   **U.** – Unity: the Body as one for the
             Audience of One - Jesus............................104
             What has to change to create a unified church
             where I worship and serve?

Chapter 6   **E.** – Evangelism: through one's life,
             ministry and mission................................. 114
             Does my church have a heart to reach beyond
             its walls?

ACKNOWLEDGEMENTS

"R.E.S.C.U.E." is dedicated to the four
most influential women in my life:
My wife, Lee, for her faithful partnership
in ministry with me;
My mother, Betty Sadler, who faithfully prayed
for me until her homecoming this year;
My mother-in-law, Mary Ann Arrington,
for her faithful encouragement;
Nancy Ryalls, my sister, for her example
of faithful discipleship to women.

Great Appreciation

John Deizo for editing my manuscript;
Jackie Krehbiel for the book cover design.
To the five Baptist churches I served, I thank the
Lord for the grace to journey in faith with you.
GRACE2U!

PREFACE

On April 10, 1912, one of the world's most massive and luxurious ships left the Southampton, England, port for New York on its maiden voyage. There was excitement surrounding this new vessel as well as pride. It was said of the *RMS Titanic* that not even "God could sink the ship," and the owners displayed their arrogance by the lack of an adequate number of life boats to accommodate the passage register. Most know the statement to be absurd. On the evening of April 14, four days into the voyage, the enormous ship glanced off an iceberg ripping into its lower deck. Within hours, the ship sank killing 1523 passengers and crew, leaving 705 survivors, and despite warnings from various sources, the luxury liner continued blindly through the frigid North Atlantic towards its demise. Years of planning through the vision, the implementation of her construction, the hiring of a crew, and the fare to board vanished into the ocean's grave yard. One man's dream finally was captured on blueprints, and then made visible as the rivets began holding the design together. One man's idea became a brief reality when the *Titanic* was buried beneath a cold star -lit evening in the North Atlantic.

Like the *Titanic* designer, Thomas Andrews, I wanted to make an impact on my culture. My dream design was building a church to win the world for Jesus. A noble vision wouldn't you say? The idea was birthed about two years after my new birth. When I was born again, the Lord changed my passion from being a college basketball coach to becoming a preacher. The vocation crossroads came when I was offered the head basketball coaching position at my high school alma mater, at the same time that the Lord was pressing my spirit towards the preaching ministry. The Lord's placing the call on my life would wake me in the wee hours of the morning. I would go into our bathroom, place my Bible on the sink and begin preaching – softly of course, because my wife was still sleeping. That was thirty-three years ago, four churches served, and my dark hair changed to a crown of gray for my services. Presently, I have recently retired from my last church, and the Lord has led me into the Transitional or Transformational Pastor (TP) ministry. By His grace, He wants to use my twilight ministry years to assist churches through their struggles.

I have admired pastors who have written about church health. My library is filled with the friends I have made through reading and implementing some of their ideas. I have valued their insights by gleaning from their research and their ministry experiences. I will introduce to you many of them through my referencing of their works. My prayer in writing this book is to complement the volumes that have already been written on the subject of church health. R.E.S.C.U.E. is the format the Lord has given me to help lead churches towards recovery. I have seen too many churches and pastors set their ministry sail towards worthy ministry goals only to see their sails ripped apart by church storms. And, yes, I've witnessed these churches unravel and sometimes sink before my eyes. Churches and pastors, like the visionaries of the infamous *Titanic*, have their ministry dreams become a vanishing reality. Hopefully, this work will help navigate churches and pastors away from destructive icebergs. As any minister and astute church member gaze upon the sea of churches, they realize this sea is dotted with icebergs of various shapes and sizes waiting for the church to collide into them. In order to continue to advance the kingdom of God, I pray the Lord give His called leaders wisdom, courage, and perseverance to steer their churches away from these icebergs. Hopefully, this life preserver or life boat called R.E.S.C.U.E. can assist your fellowship from sinking into the church sea graveyard.

INTRODUCTION

Navigating Past the Church's and Pastor's Icebergs

The Apostle John writes: "By this we know that we have come to know Him, if we keep His commandments.⁴ The one who says, "I have come to know Him," and does not keep His commandments, is a liar, and the truth is not in him;⁵ but whoever keeps His word, in him the love of God has truly been perfected. By this we know that we are in Him: (I John 2:3-5). John is simply saying be authentic. Robert Lewis states in *The Church of Irresistible Influence*, "Our postmodern world is tired of words. It wants real. Real everything. Real is convincing."[1]

The compelling force behind this book is to encourage the church and the pastors of the church to be real. Lack of authenticity is an iceberg into which too many churches collie. My confession is that I have not been *real* all the time in the three decades of ministry. The weight of pride dogged me. Lust gripped my flesh; materialism warped my mind to think I deserve the best and biggest. At times I thought more highly of myself than I should. When my son's teenage friends would be acting "all bad," he would tell them, "You are not all that."

---

[1] Robert Lewis, *The Church of Irresistible Influence*, (Grand Rapids, Michigan: Zondervan Publishers, 2001), 1.

One of my seminar professors taught that sin is our *selfish independent nature.* Clergy and church member's selfish independent nature has created a critical eye from the world.

My confession is to say, I am not all that. When I think I am, then I fall victim to Satan's temptations. Chuck Swindoll's sermon illustration of sin and its consequences has been riveted into my mind. He preached that riding the wave of sin is enjoyable and fun. We shout to the bystanders, "Look at me!" Few realize that the wave of sin will eventually crash onto the beach of consequences. I believe too many churches and pastors have crashed onto this beach. The consequence is that the world is no longer listening to our message. We have become unbelievable. The clarion call is to the preacher in the pulpit and to the parishioner in the pew to be genuine. This trumpet sound is calling us to cease riding the wave of sin. In other words, repent! Depend on God's grace!

The good news is Jesus will forgive and heal our churches and pastors. John writes, "If we confess our sins, He is faithful and righteous to forgive us our sins and to cleanse us from all unrighteousness" (I John 1:9). Ezra writes the most quoted verse about restoration, "And My people who are called by My name humble themselves and pray and seek My face and turn from their wicked ways, then I will hear from heaven, will forgive their sin and will heal their land" (II Chronicles 7:14). Can the pastors and their churches be like Nehemiah? He heard of the destruction of his city, Jerusalem, "When I heard these words, I sat down and wept and mourned for days; and I was fasting and praying before the God of heaven" (Nehemiah 1:4). Nehemiah continued in his prayer to confess the nation's sin before God. Can we begin to intercede for each other's churches? If Jesus is Lord of your church, then I encourage you to pray for revival not only for your church but also for churches across America. Yes, the church is missing the mark. How can the church hit the target of being authentic to a lost world? It is "said of the Puritans in American history that they lived as if they stood before an *Audience of One* - Jesus."[2] The church's authenticity is grounded in its motivation to glorify Jesus. The Apostle Paul wrote the foundational text for clergy and laity; "So, whether you eat or drink, or whatever you do, do all to the glory of God" (I Corinthians 10:31). Now this is a weighty passage. As one digs into the text several clear truths are stated that will make the Body of Christ believable. *Whatever I do?* This means I have to be kind, loving, forgiving, patient, not angry, not a gossip or a slanderer. I am called to go the extra mile and to turn the other cheek, and to pray for those who persecuted me. Wow! If we would live this way as Christians, I know that those on the other side of our stained glass windows or those beyond our walls might think we indeed have a meaningful message. To glorify the Lord is to display Him. Our glorifying Him makes God believable. My mother at four o'clock in the afternoon would say to my brothers and me, "Your father is coming home soon so clean up while I put my face on." I always thought the phrase, "put my face on," was odd. I thought, who have I been

---

[2]   Dallas Willard, The Divine Conspiracy, (San Franciso, California, HarperCollins Publisher, Inc., 1998), 190.

looking at all day? Before mirrors were put in car visors my wife would always turn the rear view mirror to check out her face. Then when we would meet friends for dinner, the first thing the wives would do was to excuse themselves to go powder their noses and check on their make-up. My mother, my wife, and our friend's wives wanted to show off their faces for their husbands. The church needs to be concerned how it looks before a watching world. Are we showing Jesus through our lives in a positive way?

I shared earlier that I have served four churches in three decades. After retiring, I am now serving my first official church as a Transitional Pastor or TP. Each church served was different in size and demographics. My first (Church A) was a small suburban church. The church started with twenty, and we reached the capacity for additional growth. The next ministerial venue (Church B) was a rural church of around three hundred members. From the rural setting the Lord sent us to a large city, (Church C) where the church had eight hundred members. The last was in the community where we started (Church D). This church had a resident membership of around twenty-two hundred. What is enlightening from my ministerial experience is that the location, size, or budget didn't change the common characteristics that have made churches unauthentic. Please, know, even though some of my remarks are critical, pointed, and could cause some indigestion, that I loved, enjoyed, and praised the Lord for each service arena. In each church there still remain some close relationships, many fond memories, and a big alleluia to the Lord for allowing the opportunity to watch over so many souls. I write sharing lessons from my failures, frustrations, and successes, as well as, the failures, frustrations, and successes of each church. With that said, the first lesson I learned over three decades was no matter the size or location, the proof that we are real will become evident when the church does a gut check to evaluate the following:

R – Relationships: Reconciliation/ restoration are the keys to rebuilding relationships.

Is there someone in my fellowship whom I need to forgive, to show grace, or to love more deeply?

E – Evaluation and Expectations:

Evaluation: What truly is the reality of my church?

Expectations of Staff and Members:

Staff: Called or hired staff? Members: Ministers or Pew voters?

S – Streamlined Governance: Who leads the church?

C – Clear and Concise Vision and Mission: Directional markers for the Church.

Has the leadership provided a clear direction for the church?

U – Unity: the Body as one for the Audience of One - Jesus

What has to change to create a unified church where I worship and serve?

E – Evangelism: through one's life, ministry and mission.

Does the church have a heart to reach beyond its walls?

Why *R.E.C.U.E.* Ministry? Because of the lack of authenticity, churches the builder and boomer generations created have lost their way, as have, some of the current day churches as well.

Beside the iceberg of an unauthentic church is the iceberg of Phariseeism which accentuates unauthentic churches. These churches are handcuffed by traditions, facilities, and, yes, their idols. The Pharisaical laws are mostly unwritten but numerous. A partial list includes:

No tie - for pastors less dress;
No clapping;
No slacks worn by women;
No hymn or song lyrics on overhead screens;
No talking before worship;
No Bible version but the KJV (1611);
No long hair worn by men.

The argument for dress is that Jesus wore a seamless tunic – His best. Please, really, is this all someone has to support the Pharisaical law? Really! No clapping or drums and no words on a screen? I suggest don't read the Psalms. Add to these the so called moral *NOs* with which the churches burden folk such as:

- No consumption of alcohol;
- No smoking;
- No overweight people.

I understand the biblical mandate is not to become drunk; smoking is harmful to the body, as is being overweight. So many churches make these "no's" the standard for a holy life. My wife and I were eating out one evening, and I spotted our chairman of deacons across the restaurant. Being a friendly pastor, I made my way over to him. He jumped up to shake my hand. He then pulled me forward to say, "You own me now, I'll do anything you ask." He realized that I saw his bottle of beer on the table.

One church I served had in its constitution that a member could not drink, serve, or sell alcohol. The policy was changed when I informed them that we could not invite a waiter, a grocery clerk, or a social drinker to join the church.

I was entering a hospital to visit a church member. Sitting outside the entrance was another member of my church. From a distance I saw her smoking a cigarette. As I approached her to say "hi," she flicked the cigarette over her shoulder and then stood quickly to greet me. Oh, smoke was still exiting her mouth and nostrils. Each of these experiences reminded me of how legalistic we have become. Holiness is not achieved through these manmade laws. Sadly, the "no's" keep on flowing from the legalistic fire hydrants of churches. Church has become synonymous with "no." I believe the church has created as many rules as the Pharisees of Jesus' day. In ChurchLeaders. com, Thom Rainer states that most Christians are Pharisaical.[3] Is grace not taught or lived anymore?

---

[3] Thom Rainer, *ChurchLeader Newsletter*, (http://www.church leader.com, (May 13, 2013).

Besides the Pharisaical iceberg is the *PB* or power broker iceberg. Who is in charge of the church? Who is the church boss? Bully church bosses have destroyed pastors and congregations. H.B. London who was the pastor for pastors for the "Focus on the Family" ministry stated at a pastor's conference that too many churches have "joy suckers." They suck the joy out of the church. They enjoy a good fight. It has been said of Baptists that they love food and a good fight. Shame on us, for this truly makes our churches not authentic to the watching world.

I have been amazed over the years that lay leaders think they know more than the pastor. Even if the pastor has years of education and experience, many lay leaders still believe they can lead better than the pastor. Whether single or married, a pastor worth his salt, lives for the church as he cares for his wife and children. He is praying, reflecting, and visioning for the Lord's guidance and will for the church. Most laity have jobs, families, and recreational activities that prevent them from a single focus. The church bully either has low self-esteem, feels unimportant at home, or is simply arrogant and prideful. Sadly, it becomes his way or the highway. The mindset of the church controller is that I will just outlast the pastor. I was here first; this is my church, so I will wear the pastor down.

The power broker shows his hand fairly quickly. In one church the wife in the power family said to me, "I'll scratch your back if you will ours." In another church, the long time PB's came to me to encourage me to follow their procedures to the letter. To add to the list, one couple wanted me to fire two staff ministers. These were huge givers. I didn't, and they left the church with their money.

On the flip side, PB's can be a wonderful ally. When the pastor and the PB's are not out to have their way but truly to influence the church for God's glory, then the church can flourish. This is one reason why Church C's congregation was able to build a new sanctuary and an educational/ administration building.

Lack of authenticity, Phariseeism, power brokers, and other icebergs are highlighted in the upcoming chapters.

R.E.S.C.U.E. Ministry is designed to assist churches in advancing the kingdom of God in order to glorify the Lord. As referenced earlier, the Bible is clear that in all that we do we are do glorify Jesus (I Corinthians 10:31). I pray that the implementation of R.E.S.C.U.E. will honor our Lord through the healing of your church. Remember, your community is watching to see if you are real. Francis Chan stated in his book, *The Forgotten God*, "If we have the Holy Spirit living in us, don't you think we would act differently than those who do not have the Holy Spirit?"[4] R.E.S.C.U.E. will help evaluate a church and a pastor to see if they are walking differently than those without the Holy Spirit. R.E.S.C.U.E. can be the navigational instrument to steer a church away from approaching icebergs. I pray that those who read the upcoming chapters will listen to the Spirit's leading as to what needs to be evaluated, and then,

---

4   Frances Chan, *Forgotten God*, (Colorado, Springs: David C. Cook, 2009), 32.

have the courage to make the necessary changes. Be honest, real, searching for the true reality of your church. I believe that if churches will not make honest assessments of where they are in this sea of churches that they will sink as the *Titanic*. Almost a hundred years ago those in charge of the *Titanic* didn't listen to the warnings, and they allowed their pride to sink their ship. Please approach the pages ahead humbly and prayerfully as you search for the reality of your church. The kingdom of God desperately needs you to stay afloat to impact locally, nationally, and globally the gospel of grace as taught by Jesus and the Spirit led writers of Scripture.

CHAPTER 1

*Institutions ultimately rise and fall on the
strength of relationships. When relationships
are volatile, sparks can ignite a firestorm.*[5]

R.

**Relationships: Restoration/reconciliation are
the keys to rebuilding relationships**

Restoration – rebuilding relationships within the body.
"The act of restoring or state of being restored, as to a former
or original condition, place ..." is Webster's definition. The
television show *This Old House* is about taking old houses
and restoring them to function in a more modern and efficient
manner. Like the restored house the born-again person now
fulfills his created function. The Word of God in concert with
the Holy Spirit takes our old hearts and does a makeover so
we can live for the glory of Jesus and not ourselves. Sadly,
over time many Christians have become stiff-necked in their
behavior and changeless in their methodologies. Restoration of
member's hearts is needed so healing with other individuals in

---

[5] Ron Susek, *Firestorm: Preventing and Overcoming Church
Conflict*, (Grand Rapids, Michigan: Baker Books, 2006), 30.

1

the church can honor the Lord. Then the church can advance the kingdom of God. The Apostle Paul's constant theme is to build-up one another and to encourage each other in the faith. The below process describes relationship healing:[6]

The Spiritual Cycle of Healing

A fractured relationship to a restored relationship comes through…

- Confrontation: Assertion, Compassion, and Redemption;
- Communication: Hear, Feel, and Understand;
- Forgiveness: Desire, Choice, and Release;
- Reconciliation: Negotiate, Restructure, and Fellowship

Restoration happens through reconciliation. "The act of causing two people or groups to become friendly again after an argument or disagreement" is the definition by Webster. The process displayed shows the pattern for healing: "Confrontation, Communication, Forgiveness, and Reconciliation." Most relationships remain severed because people run from confrontation. When the people of God in a church come together, then the church can be restored to accomplish its task as assigned by the Lord. Paul states in II Corinthians 5:17f

---

[6]   LifeWay Christian Resources, *Transitional Pastor Ministry Training Manuel,* (Nashville, Tennessee: LifeWay Press, 2009), 53.

we are new creations, and we have been given the ministry of reconciliation. Reconciliation ministry begins when the church is together as one. Restoration and reconciliation are the foundations of a church if it is to see relationships flourish to magnify the church's existence to glorify the *Audience of One* – Jesus.

LOVE is the vehicle in which restoration and reconciliation are transported. The new commandment given by Jesus in the Upper Room discourse ends with the command to love. Loving one another is the proof that we are disciples of Jesus. Jesus taught prior to the Upper Room event the Great Commandment: "...you shall love the Lord your God with all your heart and with all your soul and with all your strength and with all your mind, and our neighbor as yourself" (Luke 10:27). I John is a commentary on the Great Commandment. In short, I John states if we cannot love one another, then we really don't love God. If church folk cannot reconcile or be restored, then one must ask, do they really know God?

Jesus confronted our sin on the Cross. His confrontation of our sin communicated His love for us. Forgiveness came to us through His shed blood which covered our sins and turned the wrath of God from us (propitiation). Jesus forgiveness cleansed us. In our cleansing of sin which gives us the position of holiness makes us reconciled with the Lord. Now we are one with Him. In light of our being reconciled with God through Jesus, then we are to forgive and be reconciled with one another.

Secretariat, the Triple Crown winner in 1973, illustrates the meaning of *fervent love* as I Peter 4:8 describes. The word *fervent* means to strain, stretch out, or lean into. Secretariat in each win of the three famed horse races demonstrated this biblical term. In the Kentucky Derby and the Preakness, he stretched out ahead of Sham his furious competitor by 2.5 lengths. At the Belmont in New York, he captured the Triple Crown by beating Sham by 31 lengths. In each race Secretariat stretched out, leaned forward, with each stride being an energetic strain to win. Likewise, the Christian is to win the love of another by mirroring the 1973 Triple Crown winner – stretch out love to capture the heart of a brother or sister as Jesus demonstrated for us.

What are the barriers that exhaust love's energy to restore a relationship? Here are three common ones:

- Unforgiveness
- Pharisaical attitudes
- Gracelessness

Unforgiveness

Unforgiveness is the cancer in the church. When a Christian cannot forgive a brother or sister in Christ, one has to wander if this church member is truly redeemed. Could the individual not be born-again? Jesus was crystal clear from His teachings from the Sermon on the Mount: "For if you forgive others their trespasses, your heavenly Father will also forgive you" (Matthew 6:14). A failure to forgive grows from a lack of unconditional love. Many within the church have an unwritten philosophy: *As long as you are committed to my ways and ideas then I will love you.* I'm amazed how many church members give their money with the ribbon of conditions tied round it. Because they cannot forgive a staff person or another leader in the church, they withhold their money. Here is the irony – then they complain about the church. Being an unforgiving person in the church is one characteristic of a Pharisee.

Pharisaical attitudes

Are there Pharisees in the church today? These are the folks who are building a house of cards on their man-made written and unwritten laws. In one church I served I didn't wear a tie one Sunday. On Monday I received a phone call stating that the pastor of this church always wears a tie at the eleven o'clock service. Too many pseudo-Christians in the pews build a religion on the "do not's." As cited earlier, not drinking alcohol is the huge law in many denominations. But slander is tolerated. Jerry Bridges' book *Respectable Sins* drives the point home of highlighting the bigger sins while winking at the so called little sins. Churches today are pushing the 613 laws the Pharisees created to keep the Ten Commandments. Their procedural documents for the church are studied, memorized, and followed more than Scripture. If someone doesn't adhere to the law of the church, he will face an immediate reprimand. As one reads the Gospels he will find Jesus speaking more harshly to the lawmakers. These church goers have designed for themselves a hotel for pseudo saints instead of a hospital for sinners, and, some have even become the church boss or bully.

Charles Dickens once spent a year or so visiting churches in London. Dickens' essay, "City of London Churches," written in 1860 ten years prior to his death, tells the tales of those visits — the smells, the lack of congregants, the oddities of the ministers, the sleeping of those in the pews, and the sounds one hears while attending Sunday morning worship. He finishes that essay with this brilliant line about those churches: "They remain like the tombs of the old citizens who lie beneath them and around them, Monuments of another age."[7] Eventually, he became a Unitarian,

Heartbreakingly, his observations over 150 years ago remain. Examine the result of the Pharisee ruled church. One author wrote: "The main difference between congregations doomed to disband and congregations destined for revival is a willingness to adapt, to alter their congregational identity in response to change in the communities in which they are located." The author concluded, "And whether a congregation is willing to adapt depends largely on the outcome of conflict

---

[7] Charles Dickens, *The Uncommercial Traveller, City of London Churches*,(Southern Australia, University of Australia, 2013), Essay 9.

between advocates of the status quo (Pharisaical attitude) and advocates of change."[8]

Churches that were once outwardly-focused eventually become worried about the wrong things. They become more concerned about a well-used policy manual than a well-used baptistery. The Schaeffer Institute's fifteen year study shows the outcome of an inwardly focused church. Too many churches experience:[9]

- 50% of ministers starting out will not last 5 years
- 1 out 10 ministers will retire in some form of ministry
- 4k new churches start each year while 7k close each year

Here is research that we distilled from Barna, Focus on the Family, and Fuller Seminary, all of which backed up our findings, and additional information from reviewing others' research:

- Fifteen hundred pastors leave the ministry each month due to moral failure, spiritual burnout, or contention in their churches.

---

[8]   Anderson, Shawna, *Dearly Departed: How Often Do Congregations Close,* Journal for the Scientific Study of Religion, June 2008, Volume 47. 2008.

[9]   Krejcir, Richard, Schaeffer, Francis Institute, http://www.intothyword.org/apps/articles/default, **Church Growth Research Graphs and Statistics**, 2006.

- Fifty percent of pastors' marriages will end in divorce.
- Eighty percent of pastors feel unqualified and discouraged in their role as pastor.
- Fifty percent of pastors are so discouraged that they would leave the ministry if they could, have no other way of making a living.
- Eighty percent of seminary and Bible school graduates who enter the ministry will leave the within the first five years.
- Seventy percent of pastors constantly fight depression.
- Almost forty percent polled said they have had an extra-marital affair since beginning their ministry.
- Seventy percent said the only time they spend studying the Word is when they are preparing their sermons (This is Key). Most statistics say that 60% to 80% of those who enter the ministry will not still be in it 10 years later, and only a fraction will stay in it as a lifetime career. Many pastors-I believe over 90 percent-start off right with a true call and the enthusiasm and the endurance of faith to make it, but something happens to derail their train of passion and love for the call.

Of those 3,348 who felt forced to leave: These are people in a congregation:

- Sixty-one percent (61 %) of people (2,039) left their last church because of a conflict with another member resulting from gossip or strife that would not stop, was not true, or was not properly dealt with. They also marked a lack of hospitality and a lack of Bible teaching second or third, making this category 91% of significance!

- Nineteen percent, (19%) or 640 people, felt not being connected; the lack of hospitality was the number one reason. They also marked a lack of teaching second or third, and gossip also as the second or third reason. The significant factor in this category is 66%!

- Eighteen percent (18%) or 613 people said it was because of a lack of solid Bible teaching; they also marked gossip and strife and lack of hospitality as second or third.

- Four point five percent (4.5 %) or 140 people left for reasons of inconvenience; the church was too far, parking too difficult, services too long, preaching was boring, or some minor theological disagreement. It is interesting to note that this is the least of the categories for why people leave, but are what most people in church leadership and consulting spend their time and energies trying to connect with!

Bill Wilson weighs in on the topic of change referencing two words: *Resilient or Resistant.*[10] *A resilient person is receptive to change and has a mindset of flexibility. Polar opposite is the resistant individual who is inflexible and rigid towards new*

---

[10]   Bill Wilson, *Resilient or Resistant?* Center for Congregational Health, Newsletter: March 2013.

ideas. Reflecting on the below "Change Meter" diagram, where does the needle stop in your church's ability to change? Where does the needle land in your life and in your church's life?

Change Meter

The foundational aspect of change is that change will occur whether one likes it or not. Take the church building for example. If nothing is done to maintain the building it is going to change. The building will be outdated and in need of repair. Jesus came to change (transform or regenerate) the heart of man. He came to change the religious system of the Pharisees. The Bible is a life manual of how to change.

The Bible gives these four snapshots of life's changing:

- Life is swift. Job states that life is swift like a weaver's shuttle or like a runner, (Job 7:6, 9:25).
- Life is uncertain. James writes that only if it is the Lord's will he goes to this or that city, (James 4:13-16).

10

- Life change. The regenerated heart means the old has passed, and the new has come, (II Corinthians 5:17).
- Life is final. Sin brings our earthly life to an end (Genesis 3:1-3, Romans 6:23).

Each snapshot shows change. In so many areas of life we should be thankful for the changes that the Lord has allowed. I give thanks to the inventor of the microwave; I can now cook! Praise the Lord!

Gracelessness

The third barrier is lack of grace towards one another. When Christians fall into legalism or exhibit gracelessness in their relationships, these folks have forgotten their sinful nature. The self-righteous become legalists or Pharisees who are brain dead in understanding grace. Again, Philip Yancy writes, "There is nothing you can do to make God love you more and there is nothing you do to make God love you less;[11] Jerry Bridges writes, "Your worst days are never so bad that you are beyond the reach of God's grace. And your best days are never so good that you are beyond the need of God's grace."[12] This is grace. Our salvation, ministries, and yes our

---

[11]   Philip Yancey, *What's So Amazing About Grace?*, (Grand Rapids, Michigan, Zondervan Publishing House, 1997), 70.

[12]   Jerry Bridges, *The Discipline of Grace*, (Colorado Springs, Colorado, 1994), 18.

entire lives flow from God's grace towards us. People who have experienced God's grace give grace. In fact, for the past twenty years when I welcome folk to church during the worship service, I always start by saying, "Grace to you." They respond by saying, "Grace to you!" My life verse is I Corinthians 15:10 – "But by the grace of God I am what I am, and his grace toward me was not in vain. On the contrary, I worked harder than any of them, though it was not I, but the grace of God that is with me." I need grace from the congregation, and they need grace from me. I'm imperfect, and they are imperfect. Love is shown for each other by giving grace to one another. Why is this not practiced in congregations?

Here is the root of understanding grace. You understand the depth of your sin. Oswald Chambers writes, "No man knows what sin is until he is born again; the evidence that I am delivered from sin is that I know the real nature of sin in me."[13] John Newton expressed it this way, "Although my memory's fading, I remember two things very clearly: I am a great sinner and Christ is a great Savior."[14]

Congregations sing *Amazing Grace* with gusto, but few who sing the famous hymn practice grace. In the space below, draw a triangle: Write "God, the Father" at the apex; at right angle write "identity;" at left angle write "obedience." On the left side of the triangle write "Law" and on the right side write

---

[13]   Oswald Chambers, *My Utmost for His Highest*, (New York, New York, Dodd, Mead, and Company, 1935), December 26, 361.

[14]   John   Newton   Quotes: http://www.goodreads.com/author/quotes/60149.John_Newton

"Grace." Now draw a line from "obedience" to "identity." Then draw a line from "obedience" to the "Father." Most Christians believe their identity starts with obedience to the law. Thus, God is pleased with them. On the grace side of the triangle draw a line from the Father to identity. Now draw a line from identity to obedience. Mature Christians believe the Father has given them their identity through regeneration. Thus, they desire to obey the Father. We live under a covenant of grace and not the law.

Were you surprised when God regenerated your heart? A man who was an alcoholic stated that Jesus did a miracle in his life. He would tell friends that turning water into wine was nothing compared to the miracle in his life. The man said Jesus turned his whiskey into food for the family, gifts for the children, and peace throughout his home.

Barriers of unforgiveness, Pharisaical attitudes, and lack of understanding grace have caused too many churches to be institutions instead of missionary outposts. These churches have become rule keepers instead of peacemakers. A.W.Tozer in his work *Rut, Rot or Revival* describes churches as rotting because of their being memorized by routine.[15] Routine causes the people not to believe they need to change, or improve their relationship with Jesus or others. Life becomes an *unattended garden*.[16] The church stands or falls on relationships. Jesus died on a cross for us two thousand years ago so that He could have a relationship with those sheep who hear His voice. He died to give us life through Him.

Isn't it amazing that church folk share together at the Lord's Table then leave the table with animosity towards others within the church?

Jesus' teachings describe His followers. His followers are called disciples. Jesus is crystal clear about the characteristics of a disciple. First, a disciple is a Christian, and a Christian is a disciple. Understanding who we are begs the question, "What do we look like?" Jesus gives these descriptions:

- A disciple abides in the Word – John 8:31
- A disciple abounds in love - John 13:34 - 35
- A disciple bears abundant fruit – John 15:8
- A disciple abandons himself to take up his cross – Luke 9:23

My beloved, do you see yourself as a disciple? Restoration and reconciliation can only happen when these disciple attributes are visible. Chuck Colson, founder of Prison Fellowship, coined

---

[15] A.W. Tozer, *Rut, Rot, or Revival,*(Camp Hill Pennsylvania, Wing Spread Publishers, 1993), p.23.

[16] Ibid., 90.

the phrase "making the invisible kingdom visible."[17] The church makes the kingdom of God visible when it fulfills its ministry mandate – the ministry of reconciliation. The Apostle Paul writes:

> "Therefore, if anyone is in Christ, he is a new creation. The old has passed away; behold, the new has come. [18] All this is from God, who through Christ reconciled us to himself and gave us the ministry of reconciliation; [19] that is, in Christ God was reconciling the world to himself, not counting their trespasses against them, and entrusting to us the message of reconciliation. [20] Therefore, we are ambassadors for Christ, God making his appeal through us. We implore you on behalf of Christ, be reconciled to God. [21] For our sake he made him to be sin who knew no sin, so that in him we might become the righteousness of God" (II Corinthians 5:17-21).

As Christian ambassadors, representing our homeland, heaven, reconciliation is one of the high-water marks of our lives. If you have been reconciled to God through Christ, then your life is to reconcile others to Christ by being united with your brothers and sisters in Christ. Thus, we must forgive,

---

[17]   Chuck Colson: http://www.colsoncenter.org/the-center/columns/talking-points/16852-the-visible-invisible-kingdom

abandon any Pharisaical attitude, and show God's grace to each other.

David, shepherd boy then king, described for us God's sovereignty over His church and us. Most know Psalm 23 from hearing it at the majority of funerals and through sermons. The first three verses are key in the church's restoration and reconciliation. David recognizes that the LORD is sovereign by referencing God as our Master and Manager of life. Yes, Jesus is the Good Shepherd, and we shall not lack anything. David's pastoral Psalm points us to what he also understood - God's sufficiency. If you are angry, have ill will, or simply hate someone, come to this Psalm. Preacher of yesteryear, Charles Allen wrote *God's Psychiatry*. His prescription for the down cast was to read Psalm 23 five times a day for seven days.[18] Jesus promises nourishment in the green grass – His Word. He promises rest beside the sanctuary of the quiet waters. Dallas Willard in his book *The Divine Conspiracy* writes, "The key to the Christian life is to ruthlessly eradicate hurry from your life."[19] Peterson in his translation of the Bible, *The Message*, expands Matthew 11:28-30 this way:

> "Are you tired? Worn out? Burned out on
> religion? Come to me. Get away with me and
> you'll recover your life. I'll show you how to

---

[18] Charles Allen, *God's Psychiatry*, (Grand Rapids, Michigan. Baker Publishing Group, 1955), 15.

[19] Dallas Willard, *Divine Conspiracy*, (San Francisco, California, Harper Collins Publishing, Inc., 1998, p315

take a real rest. Walk with me and work with me—watch how I do it. Learn the unforced rhythms of grace. I won't lay anything heavy or ill-fitting on you. Keep company with me and you'll learn to live freely and lightly."

Don't you feel relaxed after reading this verse? Refreshment beside the still waters! The byproduct of being in the Word and in the sanctuary of rest in Jesus is a restored soul. David knows it is only the Lord who can restore a soul. As a shepherd, he would have to help sheep when they were cast down in a divot in the pasture. Christians, who are sheep, can become cast down. Obviously, one not in a relationship with Christ is cast down. Deceased pastor Ray Stedman shared a sign he saw as he crossed into Alaska, "Choose your rut carefully for you will be in it for the next 200 miles."[20] The cast down person lives in the rut of being an unforgiving person, or the Pharisee, or the one who shows little or no grace. Again, this is why Paul writes to be reconciled with Christ. Only Jesus can bring you out of the mire or the rut in your life. He restores your soul. It is the restored person whom He leads on the path of righteousness for His name sake. Ponder the words of E.M. Bounds:

"What the church needs today is not more or better machinery, not new organizations or more novel methods. She needs men whom the Holy Spirit can use-men of prayer,

---

[20] Chuck Swindoll, *The Church Awakening: An Urgent Call for Renewal,* (New York, New York, Faith Words, 2010), 30.

men mighty in prayer. The Holy Spirit does not flow through methods, but through men...He does not anoint plans, but men-men of prayer!"[21]

Being in a relationship with Christ means that He now promises to restore you through making you lie down in green pastures and leading you beside still waters. If a down cast Christian cannot be reconciled, then one must wonder about His redemption. Jesus makes it clear; a disciple is recognizable by his abiding in the Word, his love, his fruit, and his willingness to carry his cross. When a disciple is exhibiting these qualities, then the Holy Spirit is not quenched. The river of living water will not be dammed, the flame will not be smothered, nor the oil wasted. The work of restoration and reconciliation flows from the Holy Spirit actively working in the believer's life. He is a person. When we quench Him (I Thessalonians 5:19), then we grieve Him (Ephesians 4:30). His grief, anguishing over our sin, disables His work in our lives. We don't lose our salvation, but we cease to have sweet fellowship with Him. He has moved into our lives to create a residence, a home that is pleasing to anyone who crosses our path. He teaches us as we abide in the Word; He deepens our love for others, He sweetens our fruit - the nine characteristics as described in Galatians 5:22; and He selects, equips, and motivates us in service. Thus, He fulfills His purpose in glorifying Jesus (John 16:14). Here are the three T's in Scripture that will prevent the Holy Spirit from being quenched in our lives.

---

[21]   Ibid., 24.

1. **Trust** the Lord in all your life circumstances.

   - And those who know your name put their **trust** in you, for you, O LORD, have not forsaken those who seek you (Psalm 9:10).
   - Some **trust** in chariots and some in horses, but we **trust** in the name of the LORD our God (Psalm 29:7).

2. **Thank** the Lord in all your life circumstances (I Thessalonians 5:18; Ephesians 5:20).

   - ...**in everything give thanks**; for this is God's will for you in Christ Jesus.
   - **Always giving thanks** for all things in the name of our Lord Jesus Christ to God, even the Father

3. **Train** yourself in godliness (I Timothy 4: 7-8).

   - But have nothing to do with worldly fables fit only for old women. On the other hand, **discipline yourself** for the purpose of godliness; [8] for bodily discipline is only of little profit, but godliness is profitable for all things, since it holds promise for the present life and *also* for the *life* to come.

Conclusion

No church can be rescued unless the people of that church desire to be restored through reconciliation. The transitional pastor, current pastor, or interim pastor must continue to lead the people in this direction. The church can be restored, can be transformed, or can emerge when restoration and reconciliation are continually on the member's radar. You might be saying, "I cannot do this." You are right! Paul wrote that sometimes he did things he didn't want to do (Romans 7). However, in Romans 8 he replaces the pronoun I which he used twenty-seven times in chapter seven with the word Spirit in chapter eight. Seventeen times he references the work of the Holy Spirit in his life. The Spirit gives victory over chapter seven. This is why many theologians call Romans 8 the brightest gem in the treasure chest of Scripture. The jewel shines brightly on the Cross:

Condemnation debited from the believer's life account - v1
Righteousness credited to the believer's life account – v3-23
Overflowing grace towards the believer– v28 (Romans 5:20)
Sanctification process matures the believer–v30
Security in the inseparable relationship – v39

The Holy Spirit's working in a life makes reconciliation between individuals and groups possible in the church. If this does not happen, then the church will continue to decline and possibly sink into the sea graveyard of churches. Pride wins, grace loses.

CHAPTER 2

Spiritual leadership is moving people onto God's agenda.[22]

E.

Evaluation and Expectations

Evaluation

***Blood tests check the body's reality; likewise,
honest evaluations are the church's reality test.***

A thorough evaluation of the church will reveal if the church is on God's agenda. One of the first tasks of the new pastor or transitional pastor is to define the current reality of the church. Evaluation of the history of the church can help in mining for the reality. What were the most memorable moments of the church? What were the valley seasons of the church? What were the ingredients that made the "good days" good? What were the components that made the "bad days" bad?

---

[22] Henry and Richard Blackaby, *Spiritual Leadership,* (Nashville, Tennessee, Broadman & Holman Publishers, 2001), 20.

The new leader in the church can see things that the current leadership and congregation cannot see. What should be placed on the examination table? Thom Rainer in his book *Breakout Churches* writes, "Good churches do not become breakout churches until the leaders confront reality. And most church leaders are unable or unwilling to confront reality."[23]

The television show, *Kitchen Nightmares*, has the restaurant guru star, Gordon Ramsey, confronting restaurant owners as to why their businesses are failing. Ramsey reviews everything from the sight and taste of the poor quality of food to seeing the out dated appearance and atmosphere of the restaurant. Despite the decline of revenue and employee dissatisfaction, almost without exception, the owner believes his food and facility appearance are pleasing to his customers. The owners have made their tradition of running their businesses an idol. In most episodes of the program, Ramsey is able convince the owner to change his menu and the appearance of the restaurant. The end results from changing are more satisfied and repeat customers. Ramsey had to break the idols for the owners to see the reality.

Likewise, new church leadership will discover the church's idols. John Calvin stated that the heart is an idol factory.[24] Individuals and churches manufacture idols. An idol is anything you put before the face of God. The first of the Ten Commandments states, "You shall have no other gods before

---

[23] Thom Rainer, *Breakout Churches*, (Grand Rapids, Michigan Zondervan Publishers, 2005), 69.

[24] Elyse Fitzpatrick, *Idols of the Heart*, (Phillipsburg, New Jersey, P&R Publishing Company, 2001), 33.

Me;" or before My face. Idols capture our attention, resources, and time. These are even the good things in life. Our God is a jealous God. He will not have anything other than Himself be first in our lives. Idols are one of the more frequent topics addressed in Scripture.

One church I served made its historic building an idol. The powers of the church would not relocate to a nearby school. Even though the church outgrew the facility, moving to a new location for worship was out of the question. A second church's idols were its documents and money. Early in my ministry I learned that the documents usurped the Bible. Within a few months of the beginning of my nine year tenure, I stood in a meeting and informed the committee that its governing system was flawed. Only by God's grace did I stay there as long as I did. Three of the four churches I served as lead pastor were transitional churches. In my first official transitional church, its idol was its school. Everything was sacrificed to keep the school afloat, including terminating of the staff retirement for a season.

One knows something is an idol when the person or group cannot break away from it. One church could not break away from its building, another couldn't abandon its long standing documents; and another could not relegate a school to its proper place.

To evaluate or assess the situation is key in moving the church forward. The old adage, "If you keep doing the same thing and getting the same results, you might want to change." Change is what the new leadership brings into church. Change is what Blackaby hoped to inspire when he wrote about moving people (the church) onto God's agenda. Without a move towards change the church will remain in a rut. And as Tozer writes, a church that remains in a rut will eventually rot.[25]

Again, relationship building is paramount in navigating change. If relationships are fractured, a change will probably complete the break in the relationship, and more than likely church members will be on opposite sides of an issue.

In order to move folks of faith towards God's agenda, leaders need to identify the current reality through several avenues of investigation.

- Talk to people on both sides of issues. When I came to my first TP ministry the chatter from the leadership was that the current staff needed to be fired. The church could but afford two full time pastors. After talking with folks on both sides of the issue, I learned that the pastors were not the problem, but the school-idol was the thorn in the flesh.

- Read the documents. In two churches I served the documents told the story of the church. In one church the documents were the idol of the church. In fact, my reading of the documents uncovered that they had no scriptural support. What does that tell you? Maybe the Bible is not that important in leading the church or individuals. Another example, church documents

---

[25] A.W. Tozer, *Rut, Rot, and Revival,* (Camp Hill, Pennsylvania, Wing Spread Publishers, 1993), 29.

revealed an environment of legalism. They listed all the "big" sins but omitted the so called "little" sins.

- Read the history. Evaluation of the history of the church can help in unearthing the reality. What were the most memorable moments of the church? What were the valley seasons of the church? What were the ingredients that made the "good days" good? What were the components that made the "bad days" bad? Through history reading I discovered that an idol of one of the churches I served was its rich heritage in the denomination and family association. Another church split some years ago over the conservative resurgence. In reading another church's history, I found that the church split over the charismatic issue. Still another church was paralyzed because of its being a "family church."

- Who are the power brokers and bullies? These individuals show themselves fairly quickly. In my second church the power brokers were obvious, because most people shared what they said about an issue. In fact, I had to ask the person whose name was on the pastor's study door to slow down her power agenda. Power brokers usually want to talk with the pastor or leadership as well. On the other hand, the church bully holds his cards more closely. He won't reveal his hand until he extremely disagrees with the leader. Most times the power broker and bully are friendly until their ideas or suggestions are not met. One man wanted me to preach only from the KJV. Of course I didn't because I stand with the NASB or ESV. However, the rumor mill had it that I never listen to anyone. I listen; I didn't always do what they asked me to do. They eventually left the church as did others in previous churches.

- Talk with current staff. Staff can give insights that the congregation cannot. However, you must balance what the staff expresses with what the congregation expresses. Most times it is the congregation at odds with the staff, usually over leadership and direction of the church. The pastor or TP must be up front with the staff as well. I shared with one staff that it made a logistical mistake in promoting a new ministry. The staff's communication was not in sync within itself nor with the congregation. Their new ministry became a huge stumbling block for many.
- Talk with denominational leaders. Many churches are in a local association or have a field representative. Talk with these leaders to gain their perspective about the church.

Evaluation is one key in moving the church forward and into change. Understanding the current reality can assist the pastor in determining what text to preach; what individual and group meetings he needs to attend; and how fast or slowly he should navigate the church towards a fresh future. No church is the same. One cannot "cookbook" a system of how to assist churches climbing from their ruts. In the evaluation process, one must spend time in prayer, fast as the Holy Spirit leads, and be sensitive to the Holy Spirit's leadership. Remember *R.E.S.C.U.E.* is not a sequence of events, R first then on to the E, and so on, but more of Holy Spirit leadership. Restoration and Reconciliation will be on going as will evaluation. For example, in one church I was at C first before the E was addressed. Again, allow the Holy Spirit to lead! Evaluation will show the people where they have been, where they are now, and how to plan necessary steps to move onto God's agenda. The evaluation will aid in setting the expectations which flow from the Bible, the church's history, and the relationships within the church.

Expectations of Staff and Congregation

Blood tests reveal the body's problems which must be cured before setting the expectations that must be implemented in becoming healthy.

Staff Expectations:

What expectations does the congregation have of the staff?

1. To lead, to preach, to teach, to pray for, and to shepherd the flock; or
2. To be a hired hand directed by the congregation; or
3. To be a Pastor or CEO;
4. To allow the pastor to fulfill his primary mandate – to preach the Word of God?

Sadly, preaching the Word of God is not the primary expectation in most churches. A Pastor has three primary responsibilities: Shepherding, Administration, and Preaching.

The size of the font indicates the priority of the pastor, but, most often his priority is set by congregational expectations. My experiences reveal that most members desire a pastor as shepherd. However, it can be a daunting task to fulfill the expectations to visit all new church prospects, homebound, hospitalized members, and regular church members. Add to these expectations the families who are navigating the emotional trauma of a family death, couples who desire the pastor to officiate their weddings, and members who expect the pastor to oversee a family funeral. Another layer of shepherding is counseling members, and addressing conflicts within the church. Obviously, shepherding can absorb a huge amount of time.

In addition to shepherding duties there are the administration responsibilities. The pastor now has vision planning, stewardship meetings, and other administrative type gatherings. Where will the ten to twenty hours per week necessary for Bible studies and sermon preparation materialize?

Here is the crux of the pastor-congregation relationship: Is the pastor a hired hand or is the pastor the leader of the church? This will be addressed in more detail under "S" – streamlined governance.

As he examines the Biblical letters to Timothy from Paul, the preacher quickly discovers that he is to defend truth. A deposit has been given to him, and he is to guard and invest the deposit of the Gospel with his life, mainly by preaching each Sunday. To preach the Bible is the highest calling upon a pastor's life. Preaching will change lives, not shepherding or being a CEO. A pastor has to perform some of these duties, but these should not be the primary ones.

An authentic church has a pastor who spends most of his time in his study. The worn path from his study to the pulpit is obvious each week. The unauthentic church has a pastor who would rather fulfill congregational expectations than his calling to preach. Yes, this can create problems, however, if church members see the pastor placing the weight of his time in preparation and prayer, most will develop a hunger for the Word of God. Real, genuine, authentic churches have pastors who labor at their calling. There was a time in Southern Baptist life when seminaries taught potential pastors that shepherding was the key in growing a church. Shepherding might produce numbers, but a Scriptural foundation is the key to church growth, and spiritual growth of its members. Are churches preaching, teaching, and modeling the Bible as absolutely true without apology? Preaching the inerrant, sufficient view of Scripture grows the believer and, thus, the Body of Christ.

John A. Broadus pastor of First Baptist of Charlottesville, VA (1851-1859) made a sobering remark that creates a pause for churches today: "Brethren, we must preach the doctrines; we must emphasize the doctrines; we must go back to the doctrines. I fear that the new generation does not know the doctrines as our fathers knew them,"[26] If that was his fear then, how about today? Albert Molher, President of Southern Baptist Theological Seminary, in Louisville, KY, writes in *A Passionate Plea for Preaching,* the following:

> Luther tried to go back to the first century and understand the essential marks of the church, and the first mark he listed was preaching. Where the authentic preaching of the Word takes place, the church is there, he said. By contrast, where it is absent, there is no church. No matter how high the steeple, no matter how large the budget, no matter how impressive the ministry, it is something other than the church.[27]

The pulpit grows the membership both spiritually and numerically. Sorrowfully, most church's programs, activities, and ministries overshadow the pulpit. The church grapevine chatter is more about the "doing," rather than discussing what was heard from the pulpit. I heard Pastor David Jeremiah via the radio challenge churches either to grow the church with programs or with the Word of God. People are searching for truth. Mission endeavors are great, but they are subpar if the

---

[26] John Broadus Quotes: http://www.swordofthelord.com/biographies/BroadusJohn.htm

[27] R. Albert Mohler, Jr., *Feed My Sheep: A Passionate Plea for Preaching: The Primacy of Preaching,* (Orlando, Florida, Reformation Trust Publishing, 2008), 10.

missionary brings an errant view of the Bible. Preachers who shortchange the hearers by giving them teachings that tickle their ears are only eroding the hearer spiritually.

Having ministered in four churches of different sizes, I learned that the common denominator of each church's growth was the preaching of God's Word. The preacher doesn't have to be a preacher of yesteryear like Charles Spurgeon (the Prince of Preachers) or a modern day expositor of the Word like Ed Young, Jr., Andy Stanley, or Tim Keller. Albert Molher cites three foundational principles to which every preacher should adhere to:

- Preaching must be a priority of the preacher's weekly responsibilities.
- Congregations must undertake the responsibility to guarantee that the Word is being preached.
- Expository preaching must be the format of all preachers. [28]

The hardest principle to accomplish is to make the sermon the priority of the week. The preacher's week is mixed with responsibilities of administration, counseling, visitation, and preparation for Bible teaching. One of the best strategies was from Methodist preacher Charles Allen of Huston. He shared at a Billy Graham Evangelistic Conference in the early 1980's that he would go to his study above his garage by 7:00 a.m. on

---

[28]   Ibid., 16.

Thursdays. He would not leave until he had studied, prayed, and written two sermons for the Sunday services. Saturday night specials really don't cut it. Yes, I have done them, and occasionally, the Lord blesses. Only by His grace! However, I believe that He expects us to spend hours on reflection and preparation to feed the sheep on Sunday. The pastor must make his strategy of sermon preparation a priority of his week. Also, the congregation should help the pastor make preaching a priority. I have taped to my computer screen the words of preacher Thomas Griffin (1861-1924) that a dear saintly lady in my third church gave to me. "Think yourself empty, read yourself full, write yourself clear, pray yourself keen-then enter the pulpit and let yourself go!"

The congregation will quickly notice if the preacher makes his sermon a priority. How does the preacher know if he is preaching and not tickling their ears? Trouble will surface. Congregants who are immature or not saved will not accept sound biblical preaching. They will choke or get indigestion from hearing truth. Over the years members have left, because I preached against the homosexual lifestyle or against abortion. Folks have church-shopped, because they become convicted about how they are living when faced with Scriptural instruction about holiness. Senior adult unmarried couples who lived together for financial benefits from the government have left churches I have served. One couple wanted me to officiate their marriage despite saying that one of them really didn't want a Christian marriage and home. Another couple stated they desired a Christian marriage and home but were living together.

I suggested that they separate until the wedding day in order to honor the Lord. The fiancé emailed me after the initial pre-marital counseling session saying they found another preacher to officiate their marriage ceremony. Even though individuals left each church I oversaw because of these issues, the majority of the congregation supported me. Why? They realized that the Word was being preached. Even though it made some of them uneasy, they knew they needed to hear truth. After the morning service many members over the years have said that I stepped on their toes. I would respond by saying I missed; I really was aiming for your heart! Congregations want to hear truth; so faithfully preach the Word.

What does it mean to preach faithfully the Word of God? Do expositional preaching: word by word, line by line preaching sets a feast before the people. Hopefully, each Sunday the preacher serves a gourmet meal to his congregation. Worshippers come with Bible and pen in hand ready to be fed. As the preacher preaches Scripture upon Scripture, the congregation's spiritual bellies becomes satisfied. Over the years I have found preaching through the books of the Bible to be the best way to feed the flock, eliminating speculations that I am using the pulpit to address a particular issue in the church. No one can accuse the preacher of having a "bully pulpit" or of referring to malcontents in the church. Biblical book preaching, as I call it, forces the preacher to address all doctrines. He will address easy texts as well as the challenging ones that many preachers sweep under the doctrinal rug.

How disheartening that so many preachers today only fix appetizers and desserts to serve at the Sunday service meal. No meat is prepared. Read a text, and tell a good joke, relevant stories, or a poem, and the people will love you. But they are malnourished and don't even know it. Many times the text has nothing to do with the joke, story or poem. The sermon is philosophical, rational, and social in nature. Texts that deal with sin, hell, judgment, and holy living are rarely, if ever, set on the table.

The preacher's bottom line is James 3:1; "Not many of you should become teachers, my brothers, for you know that we who teach will be judged with greater strictness." This one verse should take preachers to their knees each week. When one goes to a high-priced restaurant, he expects a quality meal to be served. In fact, the servers and waiters ask if your meat is cooked to your specifications. If the meat is not prepared to your liking, you send it back to the cook. Many a sermon should be sent back to the preacher's study. Honestly, I know I have had a few that were not prepared properly. One day though, the Lord is going to judge me by the meals I served on Sundays.

Preach the Word. Be ready to preach, so that those under your charge will come to Jesus through His amazing effectual call, and He will grow them by grace. In I Corinthians 1:21 Paul says, "God was pleased through the foolishness of what was preached to save those who believed." Yes, preaching is a foolish mystery. Even though a mystery, when the Word is preached Isaiah wrote:

"For as the rain and the snow come down from heaven and do not return there but water the earth, making it bring forth and sprout, giving seed to the sower and bread to the eater, so shall my word be that goes out from my mouth; it shall not return to me empty, but it shall accomplish that which I purpose, and shall succeed in the thing for which I sent it" (55:10-11).

The promise is people will be fed, convicted of sin, and come into a relationship with the Lord through the feast prepared for them.

John Calvin preached using the plural pronouns (we, us, our) to show his listeners that he too was on this journey of spiritual maturity.[29] The contemporary preacher must be authentic. He needs to share his struggles, frustrations, and joys. He communicates that he too is depending on the Lord as he travels on the path of righteousness. One of my weekly, *Beyond Our Walls,* articles to the church highlights this theme:.

Beyond Our Walls
The Bible: God's Surgical Instrument
Hebrews 4:12-13

Do you remember the TV series in the mid-seventies Six Million Dollar Man starring Lee Majors as Steve Austin? He was a former astronaut with bionic parts working for OSI (Office of Scientific Intelligence) upholding the law as a secret

---

[29]   Burk Parsons, Editor, Steven Lawson, *John Calvin: A Heart for Devotion, Doctrine, and Doxology,* (Orlando, Florida, Reformation Trust Publishing, 2008), 77.

agent. Austin became the six figure warrior after a plane crash. His operation cost six million dollars. His right arm, both legs and left eye were replaced by "bionic" devices which gave him super human strength, speed, and sight. Believe it or not I'm your bionic pastor. That's right! However, the buckles that hold my retinas in place and the eye implants don't have 20:1 zoom lens capability. The partial knee replacement has not increased my running speed to 60 miles per hour. Plus, my surgeon forgot to insert the bionic devices from the two thoracic surgeries which were necessary to give me super human strength. I guess I needed better health insurance. I'm your bionic pastor without Sampson like strength. But, wait a minute – I do have six million dollar power. So do you!

The Lord has performed major surgery on me and hopefully on you, as well. He is the world renowned Cardiovascular Specialist. The Bible is His sharpest surgical instrument. Hebrews 4:12 says that the Word is "shaper than any two-edged sword." When I came face to face with the Word of God, I came face to face with myself. My life was "open and laid bare" before the Lord (v13). I discovered that I was a sinner. In fact, I am a great sinner. My Heart Surgeon replaced my old sinful heart with a new heart (Ezek. 36:26). He used stitches of grace to hold my new heart in place. Now I'm a new creation with power (II Corinthians 5:17, Acts 1:8).

Our text teaches that the Word of God is "living and active." Isaiah 55:11 supports our text, "so shall my word be that goes out from my mouth; it shall not return to me empty, but it shall accomplish that which I purpose, and shall succeed in the thing for which I sent it." Did you sense the power from the verse? When the Bible is read, preached, or taught, something is going to happen. As one of my professors used to say, "When the Word is spoken, the Holy Spirit anoints the Word as it travels from your mouth to the ears of the hearer. He plants the Word in the soil of that heart." The Word is active, living, and powerful enough to perform the heart transplant surgery. The Lord takes the heart of stone and transforms it into a heart of flesh (Ezekiel 36:26). We have greater powers than Steve Austin; we have power that will change a life forever.

Examine closely this surgical tool of the Lord:

1. The Word gives spiritual insight into real life (Psalm 119).
2. The Word gives endurance to run the race of faith set before us (Heb.12:1-2).
3. Scripture gives strength to stand firm against the schemes of the devil and his workers (Ephesians 6:10f).

Now you know, my friends, disciples of Jesus have Bible power! Disciples are identified by their abiding, obedience, or continuance in the Word (John 8:31).

A Pastor's Life: Blending in or Breaking out?

Some pastors will strive to be liked by everyone in the congregation. Doctor Luke cites Jesus' warning about everyone's speaking well of you, "Woe to you, when all people speak well of you, for so their fathers did to the false prophets" (6:26). To accomplish popularity, a pastor will have to compromise many Biblical, social, and political views. Too many pastors blend into their congregations. The pastor must be a part of the body but must also be its leader. As the leader he should live a standard that leads the congregation he serves. What will separate him from the pack, so to speak? Let's examine briefly the Sermon on the Mount (Matthew 5-7).

Here we find that followers of Jesus are to pray for those who persecute them; to turn the other cheek; to walk the extra mile; to give, to fast, and to pray. This body of Scripture teaches us to love those who are different than us and to forgive others as Christ has forgiven us. Finally, the key text is 5:20 which states that our righteousness must exceed the righteousness of the scribes and Pharisees. If the pastor cannot exercise what Jesus taught, don't expect the congregation to do so either. When the Body of Christ sees the pastor hungering and thirsting after righteous, many within the flock will emulate him.

Allow me to reiterate the point of preaching the Word of God as the primary responsibility of the pastor. Preaching the Word will distinguish the pastor from the membership. Many writers and teachers have stated, "So goes the pulpit so goes the church." A congregation must realize that the church is built on the Word of God in concert with the Holy Spirit. The sword, the Word of God, is sharper than any two edged sword. The Bible is the living Word which will never wither or fade (Hebrews 4:12, I Peter 1:23-25, II Timothy 3:16). The Word will complete what it was intended to accomplish (Isaiah 55:11).

The effective preacher is empowered by the Holy Spirit through a disciplined prayer life. A prayer life is continuous and constant from the pastor's recognizing his helplessness. Prayer is for the helpless.[30] The pastor needs to communicate and demonstrate his dependency on prayer. His prayer life is evident throughout his ministry to the congregation. His private prayer life, worship prayers, and shepherding prayers indicate his total reliance on Jesus. The pastor's prayer life will enhance and enable his accomplishing our next point.

One of the primary goals of the TP is to teach the congregation a healthy view of the pastor-congregation relationship. The number one reason pastors are fired or removed is disagreement as to who is in charge of the church. The pastor is not a dictator but a servant-leader. As the under-shepherd of the flock, the pastor leads it to the Word of God so parishioners can walk the path of righteousness for the glory of the Lord. I Peter 5:1-3: "So I exhort the elders among you, as a fellow elder and a witness of the sufferings of Christ, as well as a partaker in the glory that is going to be revealed: ² shepherd the flock of God that is among you, exercising oversight, not under compulsion, but willingly,

---

[30] Paul Miller, *A Praying Life*, (Colorado Springs, Colorado, NavPress, 2009), 55.

as God would have you; not for shameful gain, but eagerly; [3] not domineering over those in your charge, but being examples to the flock." This is a wonderful text for alliteration. Unpacking the text for the congregation can aid in its understanding of the expectations it should have of its pastor.

1. The pastor's mandate: *exhorted* to shepherd v2a

The pastor's calling is to shepherd the flock. As stated, the main way in fulfilling this aspect of his responsibility is to preach expository sermons. Martin Lloyd-Jones advocates sermon counseling.[31] A member's problem or struggle can be addressed and solved by applying Biblical instruction to the situation. To shepherd is to lead. Leadership means to effect influence.

2. The pastor's ministry: *exercise* oversight v2b

Exercising oversight is providing vision with leadership to fulfill the vision. Oversight is evaluating the church to determine its health. Once the diagnosis is made, the pastor prescribes treatment for the church so it can regain its health.

---

[31]   Martyn Lloyd-Jones, *Spiritual Depression: Its Causes and Its Cure,* (Grand Rapids, Michigan, Eerdmans Publishing Company, 1983), 10.

3. The pastor's motivation: *eagerness* apart from selfish gain v2c

The pastor's willing eagerness to glorify the Lord drives him to lead the church. He is not motivated by material gain, positional notoriety, or popularity. He is before the people to honor and mirror Jesus not himself. He is decreasing, so Christ can increase (John 3:30).

4. The pastor's methodology: *example* not dictatorship v3

The congregation should expect the pastor to lead a moral life, and display humility. Peter in the text says showing humility to one another for the Lord gives grace to the humble (v5). Humility flows from a life that is dependent on the Holy Spirit. Earlier, I discussed the work of the Holy Spirit in the life of the church. The congregation must see the Holy Spirit working in the pastor's life. If congregants see his not quenching and grieving the Holy Spirit, then they will desire his walk with the Lord. For example, the pastor displays the fruit of love. If he wants the people to be on God's agenda, then he loves them like a shepherd. This doesn't mean he has to be the hired hand. No, he leads in love. As the under-shepherd, the pastor is deeply in love with the Shepherd – Jesus.

Preaching pales a distant second to the pastor's love for Jesus. The Apostle John's vision on Patmos Island reveals Jesus' heartache with the church of Ephesus. In Revelation 2 John shares Jesus' disappointment that this church had placed ministry above loving Him. Oswald Chambers touches on the point in his June 19 devotion in *My Utmost for His Highest*:

> "Lovest thou Me? . . . Feed My sheep."
> - John 21:16

> "Jesus did not say – Make converts to your way of thinking, but look after My sheep, see that they get nourished in the knowledge of Me. We count as service what we do in the way of Christian work; Jesus Christ calls service what we are to Him, not what we do for Him. Discipleship is based on devotion to Jesus Christ, not on adherence to a belief or a creed. "If any man come to Me and hate not . . ., he cannot be My disciple." There is no argument and no compulsion, but simply – If you would be My disciple, you must be devoted to Me. A man touched by the Spirit of God suddenly says – "Now I see Who Jesus is," and that is the source of devotion"(John 12:24).[32]

A more current writer Paul Tripp reiterates Chambers' thoughts that one's devotion to Jesus is paramount to any ministry. He shares his life from his book *Dangerous Calling:*

---

[32] Oswald Chambers, *My Utmost for His Highest*, (New York, New York, Dodd, Mead and Company, 1935), June 19, 171.

"Ministry had become my identity. No, I didn't think of myself as a child of God, in daily need of grace, in the middle of my on sanctification, still in a battle with sin, still in need of the body of Christ, and called to pastoral ministry. No, I thought of myself as a pastor. That's it, bottom line. The office of pastor was more than a calling and set of God-given gifts that had been recognized by the body of Christ. "Pastor" defined me. It was me in a way that proved to be more dangerous that I would have thought... In ways that my eyes didn't see and my heart was not yet ready to embrace, my Christianity had quit being a relationship."[33]

Writers from yesteryear and today mandate the paramount teaching of Scripture to love the Lord your God with all one's being. This intimate relationship can be achieved by creating time to enjoy our Creator. Intimacy is not created but must be sought purposefully.[34] During my thirty-nine years of marriage to Lee I have planned special anniversary weekends. One of the more humorous ones occurred while living in Raleigh, North Carolina. Our anniversary sometimes falls on Easter weekend. That was the case this year in Raleigh. With Easter services

---

[33] Paul Tripp, *Dangerous Calling*, (Wheaton, Illinois, Crossway Books, 2012), 27.

[34] Paul Miller, *A Praying Life*, (Colorado Springs, Colorado, NavPress, 2009), 47.

on the horizon, I planned an overnight retreat in the city. I reserved a room in an upscale hotel, packed Lee's necessities for the overnight, and then picked her up from work. As I was driving from her work, she inquired where I was going. I shared that I had a surprise for her. When I drove into the hotel parking lot, she asked, "Why are we here?" I explained that this was our anniversary get-away. She replied by saying, "We can't stay here!" With a curious look, "I asked why not?" Lee, in a high pitched voice said, "Somebody might see us!" I laughed, and then in a soft shout said, "We are married!" Well, we had a great evening and morning before returning home. As in any relationship, time must be created for the relationship. Especially our relationship with Jesus.

To cite Dallas Willard's key to the Christian's life again, he brings home the answer for creating intimacy: "The key to the Christian life is to ruthlessly eradicate hurry from our lives."[35] Most people, especially pastors, must confess that they are too busy. As someone put it, busy is **Being Under Satan's Yoke**. Not a healthy picture of the Christian life, especially when the believer is called to "Cease striving" or, "Be still" and know that I am God" (Psalm 46:10a).

The souls for whom ministers care must see their overseer in love with Jesus first and foremost. This will be the best example ministers can set for their congregations.

[35] Dallas Willard, *Divine Conspiracy*, (San Francisco, California, Harper Collins Publishing, Inc., 1998), 315

What are the staff expectations of the congregation?

Scripture mandates that the congregation must fulfill three expectations:

1. Equipped to minister : "And He gave some as apostles, and some as prophets, and some as evangelists, and some as pastors and teachers, [12] for the **equipping of the saints** for the work of service, to the building up of the body of Christ," (Ephesians 4:11-12);

2. Encourage the staff: "Therefore **encourage** one another and build up one another, just as you also are doing. [12] But we request of you, brethren, that you **appreciate** those who diligently labor among you, and have charge over you in the Lord and give you instruction, [13] and that **you esteem them** very highly in love because of their work. Live in peace with one another" (I Thessalonians 5:11-13); and

3. Submit to the called staff: "Obey your leaders and submit to them, for they keep watch over your souls as those who will give an account. Let them do this with joy and not with grief, for this would be unprofitable for you" (Hebrews 13:17).

Equip to Minister

When the Holy Spirit calls a person to follow Jesus, this person enters into the school of discipleship. As a disciple he now learns the ministry that the Lord has for him to fulfill. The word equip is a medical term meaning to put in its proper place. When a bone is broken, the doctor sets the fractured bone into its designed position. Likewise, the Word of God in concert with the Holy Spirit places Christians in various ministries to serve in the kingdom of God. Romans 12, I Corinthians 12, Ephesians 4, and I Peter 4 address the biblical mandate to serve. John MacArthur in his commentary on I Corinthians highlights the reasons for spiritual gifts being exercised by the believer:[36]

1. Edification of the church;
2. Satisfaction of the believer; and
3. Glorification of the Lord.

Edification of the Body: I Corinthians 12:7 clearly states that the variety of gifts is for the common good of the body of Christ. I Peter 4:10 exhorts the believers to use their gifts to serve each other. As the body of Christ serves one another, the watching world sees the love the members have for one other.

Satisfaction of the believer: Jesus stated that the world will know His followers by their fruit, as recorded in John

---

[36] John MacArthur, *I Corinthians Commentary*, (Chicago, Illinois, Moody Press, 1984), 293-295.

15:8. Not only does their fruit of Galatians with nine different characteristics as set out in Galatians bring satisfaction, but also it yields ministry fruit. Ministry fruit is how we serve one another. Christians are most fulfilled and fruitful when they serve. I found over the years that those who serve complain the least and trust the staff the greatest. On the other hand, if the fruit cannot be observed in the minister, then his ministry is meaningless and useless.

Glorification of the Lord: This is the motivation in our service. Service mirrors Jesus' earthly ministry. He had compassion. Not only did He feel sympathy towards others but He reached out to touch their lives as well. Peter again pens the result of one's ministry:

As each has received a gift, use it to serve one another, as good stewards of God's varied grace: as one who serves by the strength that God supplies—in order that in everything God may be glorified (Emphasis added) *through Jesus Christ. To him belong glory and dominion forever and ever. Amen* (I Peter 4:10-11).

The Chic-fil-A organization, a Christian business, set the example for the church during Atlanta, Georgia's, January 2014 winter storm. Cars, trucks, and school buses were held hostage by the icy road conditions on the city's many freeways. Folks were stranded for as much as fifteen hours in their vehicles. Employees of the Chic-fil-A restaurants in the area fixed food and served as many people as they could in their cars at no charge. Also, those who could stay in the restaurant were invited to do so. What a wonderful example for the body of Christ to edify Jesus by compassionately serving others!

Encourage the Staff

Years ago I used an illustration to highlight this point in a sermon. I cannot remember where I borrowed the story. The story is about a young pastor called to a Boston city church. The elders of the church were divided on the candidate. One elder stated that the man was too young. Another said he had no large church experience. The oldest elder stood in the meeting, paused, and then said to the others – what you have said is true. However, we can make him great. Wow! I have never forgotten this illustration. It hit home.

Elders in another church did the opposite. They were more critical and non-supportive of making things work in the church. When hate letters were written to the pastor or he was publically demeaned, the elders took no action. I believe the church elected leadership will either make or break the pastor. My sister, a wonderful children's minister, gave me a most helpful idea – an encourager file. File away all the letters, cards, and emails that were positive. When things become tough for the pastor, he can go through the file to be reminded that he is loved and appreciated.

Exemplify Submission

The most misunderstood and, yes, the most hated word today is submission. When I've done pre-marital counseling, many future brides did not like the idea of submitting or being obedient to their husbands. I find it odd that most submit to the laws of America but have difficulty submitting to Biblical teachings. I believe herein lies the problem of the church today. Read the following passages below:

> *Obey your leaders and submit to them, for they are keeping watch over your souls, as those who will have to give an account. Let them do this with joy and not with groaning, for that would be of no advantage to you* (Hebrews 13:17).

> *We ask you, brothers, to respect those who labor among you and are over you in the Lord and admonish you, and to esteem them very highly in love because of their work. Be at peace among yourselves* (I Thessalonians 5:12-13).

> *...submitting to one another out of reverence for Christ* (Ephesians 5:21).

Again, a congregation cannot lead itself. The Lord has always appointed leaders; whether political, local, home, work, or church. There are people over us. I think many churches are in the twilight zone thinking they are exempt from coming under someone's authority. As Christians we are under the authority of Scripture, the Holy Spirit, and the church leadership.

To discover why so many refuse to submit we must determine whether the congregation has a Humdudgeon or a Halleluiah attitude. A halleluiah attitude creates submission! *God's grace grasped (ICor.15:10) leads to heart-filled gratitude (IICor.4:15) that magnifies the Lord (Ps.69:30-32), which cultivates the heart for humility to grow and then humility creates the desire to submit or obey.*

Let's be honest. Why do we all struggle with submission? Is it our desire for control? Do we think we have certain rights that make us rebel against those over us? What are the by-products of such an attitude? Is our lack of submission a root cause of anxiety (I Peter 5:5-7)? Does a non-submissive attitude indicate lack of trust in the Lord (I Peter 5:6-7)? Peter answers why so many Christians are not submissive in I Peter 5:5, "God opposes the proud."

Submission flows from surrender. Most Christians exclaim for commitment. Commitment can only come through surrender of the will. The Christian surrenders to the Holy Spirit's leading – not my will but your will, Lord. Without surrender pride has the edge.

Pride stands in the wing of our heart's stage, ready to walk onto the stage of our heart to be the star. Pride displays its acting ability by our patting our foot in the long grocery line, or by our being an aggressive driver. Our opinion has to be heard, and it is always right. Sometimes we treat others as inferior to ourselves. Many cover their pride by saying,"You don't know my heart." Oh, yes, people do. We might not notice pride dancing on our hearts, but others do. It is like bad breath. Others know we have it, but we don't.

Another acting strategy of pride is self-pity. This script contains numerous times the line, "Oh poor me." Pride loves the screen play for this one. So many caring people rally to the person's aid to listen to his tragic story. I am not referring to folks who are going through an initial struggle, but to those who cannot overcome the hurt of yesterday, or who think they have been dealt an unfair hand, or who moan that someone did not treat them correctly.

Whether pride comes forth boastfully, arrogantly, or in a non-intrusive way, the spotlight still shines on the individual. This is what makes pride the star. Thus, to keep pride off the stage of our hearts one must develop a submissive attitude. Pride leads to a Humdudgeon attitude, *i.e., A loud complaint about a trifle.*[37]

T-shirt and bumper sticker slogans can often have meaningful insights. One T-shirt worn by a prideful person has this inscription: *I am my own role model.* We have buried the characteristic of respect for authority. We fail to respect those authorities over us. Peter is driving a stake of decency into the ground. If we are Christian, then our desire and delight will be to submit. I cannot be my own authority.

---

[37] Elizabeth Elliott, *Keep a Quiet Heart*, (Ann Arbor, Michigan, Servant Publications, 1995), 89.

Submission*: The ability to lay down the terrible burden of always needing to have one's own way.*[38] All the disciplines of the Christian faith are designed to set us free. Jesus came to set us free. Submission is a key disciple for freedom. People have spent weeks, months, years and, yes, decades with suppressed hurt or angry feeling, because something didn't go their way. Churches split and folks stay angry with each other for a lifetime, because they didn't get their way. Families fracture because of selfish attitudes from one's not getting his way. Every relationship has the potential of destruction because of the phrase, "I didn't get my way." All fights are caused by enslavement to having it my way. We must remember humility cultivated will produce a submissive attitude.

Jesus did not allow the actor, Pride, to take the stage in His life. How did He accomplish this submission? Submission means obedience. And obedience means that I die to myself. One finds clear submission in Jesus' life: Andrew Murray highlights these in his work, *The School of Obedience:*

1. Submission to the Father was a ***determined principle.*** John 6:38, "I came not to do mine own will." We are to live a submissive life, because Jesus lived one. He lived the "cross-life" which is a life of voluntary submission.
2. Submission to the Father was a ***delighted practice.*** John 4:34, "My food (meat) is to do the will of him who sent

---

[38]   Richard Foster, *The Celebration of Discipline*, (New York, New York, HarperCollins Publishers, 1978), 111.

me and to accomplish his work." Jesus craved doing the will of the Father.

3. Submission to the Father was **displayed patience**. Jesus never rushed. Lazarus died but Jesus didn't rush to raise him from the dead. The cross was before Him, but He allowed the Father to unfold the events that would eventually lead Him to Calvary's Hill.

4. Submission to the Father was unto **death**. Philippians 2:8, "He humbled himself by becoming obedient to the point of death, even death on a cross."[39]

At eighty-two the last words of hymn writer and pastor, John Newton were; "I am satisfied with the Lord's will." In a letter to a friend Newton describes the believer's life; "He believes and feels his own weakness and unworthiness, and lives upon the grace and pardoning love of his Lord. This gives him a habitual tenderness and gentleness of spirit." "Amazing Grace" was written to accompany a New Year's Eve sermon from I Chronicles 17:16: *Who am I, O LORD God, and what is my house that you have brought me thus far?* Those surrounded by Newton characterized him as a man of habitual tenderness.[40] Newton would summarize life as St. Augustine described it as

---

[39]   Andrew Murray, *School of Obedience*, (Chicago, Illinois, Moody Press, 1997), 31-36.

[40]   John Piper, *The Roots of Endurance: John Newton*, (Wheaton, Illinois, Crossway Books, 202), 72.

"one big halleluiah." Halleluiah defined: "A loud praise about God's amazing grace."[41]

Understanding God's grace should create a heart of gratitude. A heart of gratitude should produce a humble follower of Jesus which results in a willingness to submit. St. Augustine stated, "God always pours His grace into empty hands."[42] As Paul stated, I am what I am by grace (I Corinthians 15:10). What business man would say to the daily newspaper reporter that my success is because of the grace of God? What medical doctor at the local hospital or university professor, if interviewed by their respective journals, would say that by God's grace I am able to do this surgery or teach this subject? We are what we are by God's grace. I am here only by God's grace. Thus, I am to display God's grace (I Corinthians 15:10c). Paul stated that he worked harder, but it was not he but God's grace working through him. Even in his suffering he stated in II Corinthians 12:8 that God's grace was sufficient for him. I display God's grace by giving grace: not by condemning, slandering, or gossiping about a brother or sister. I show grace so others can be liberated from their pride, their self-sufficiency, and their being on the throne of their lives.

Donald Barnhouse who served 10th Presbyterian Church in Philadelphia wrote: "Love that goes upward is worship; love that goes outward is affection; love that stoops is grace."[43] See

41   Ibid., 80.
42   David Jeremiah, *Captured by Grace*, (Nashville, Tennessee, Integrity Publishers, 2006), 17.
43   Donald Barnhouse, http://www.publicisejesus.org/quotes.html

the picture: God stooping over heaven's edge giving the One who is full of grace and truth, Jesus, for you. We stoop to give grace to those who do not deserve it. Do you really understand what Christ has done for you?

Understanding the work of God's special grace creates heart-filled gratitude which becomes fertile soil of the heart for humility. My life is a thankful life. How do I know I have a thankful life? Andrew Murray answers the question: "Humility before God is nothing if not proved in humility before men."[44]

I will praise the name of God with a song;
I will magnify him with thanksgiving.
And it will please the Lord better than an ox
or a young bull with horns and hoofs.
The humble have seen it and are glad;
you who seek God, let your heart revive! *(Psalm 69:30–32)*

Humility and a submissive spirit are mark by a thankful attitude. Thankfulness makes God look as big as He really is. A telescope magnifies things to look as they really are. The Hubble Telescope brings us pictures from the heavens to show us the awesomeness of God's creation. A microscope makes small things look bigger. Thanksgiving is not a microscope but a telescope. When you thank God, praise Him, and give him the

---

[44] Andrew Murray, *Humility: The Beauty of Holiness,* (Fort Washington, Pennsylvania, Christian Literature Crusade, 2010), 35.

gratitude He deserves, you have magnified Him before others. Now others observe His greatness.

The Apostle Paul wanted to make thankfulness for God's grace perfectly clear to his son in the faith Timothy. Paul stated to the elders in Ephesus (Acts 20:24) that he didn't consider his life worth much in light of preaching the gospel of grace. In his first letter to Timothy, Paul shares the magnitude of grace in chapter 1:12-18.

Gratitude for His salvation – v12

St. Augustine, once Bishop of Hippo in North Africa, was the womanizer of womanizers. One day Augustine was walking through the square, and he heard a female voice, "Augustine, it is I." Augustine, seeing her, began to retreat, and as he retreated he shouted back, "Yes, but it is not I." New creation is one's status when he trusts Jesus. 2 Corinthians 5:17 states that the "...the old things passed away; behold, new things have come." The gospel changes people. The Word of God changes people. The spirit of God changes us. The blood of Christ changes us. The transformation is a new heart and a new mind that has been set ablaze by God. "Such were some of you; but you were washed, but you were sanctified, but you were justified in the name of the Lord Jesus Christ and in the Spirit of our God" (I Corinthians 6:11).

This is how I was; now look at me. Paul is saying if it were not for God's grace I would still be far from God. "We are justified by his grace as a gift, through the redemption that is in Christ Jesus" (Romans 3:24). Paul joyfully writes Timothy saying I am...

- Grateful for strength from the Lord;
- Grateful that God found me trustworthy; and
- Grateful for the service or ministry the Lord has given me.

Recipient of mercy – v13

Paul received mercy for his sinfulness against God. He stated that he was a blasphemer, a persecutor, and a violent aggressor towards God. In fact, he writes that he acted ignorantly in unbelief. He shares in his Philippians letter his pristine resume (3:2-10). His conclusion is that when compared to Christ, all of his accolades are but rubbish. When Christ enters into the equation of life, He surpasses all that we accomplish. In sin, we are ignorant in thinking that our accomplishments are worthy.

Paul said to Timothy that Paul had been granted mercy. Grace removes guilt; mercy takes away the misery caused by sin. Paul received underserved relief of misery that is packaged with saving grace. Grace gives the believer what he does not deserve. Mercy does not give what the believer deserves.

I remember one time when my dad had my brothers, Mike and Rick, and me lined up at the woodshed. We had been naughty in church. When the choir minister moved in front of the choir for the anthem, we rose from our seats and mimicked his arm motions. Three fourths of the congregation noticed our bold misbehavior. Well, this didn't set well with our father. Following our reprimand in church came the announcement of our visit to the woodshed. Arriving home, dad ordered us to go to the woodshed and remove our belts. With belts in hand, dad said with a stern voice, "Don't ever, ever do that again." He turned and walked away. I think he walked away with somewhat of a smile on his face. We didn't receive what we deserved. He granted mercy.

Abundance of grace – v14

Paul says he was flooded with grace: it was a tsunami of grace. It overflowed me! The degree which we understand our sin is the degree we will understand God's grace in our lives. As a tsunami totally changes the landscape of the land area it overflows, grace overflowed Paul's heart and changed its landscape from a heart of unrighteousness to righteousness. Through grace, God regenerated Paul's heart to have faith to follow Jesus. Grace taught Paul *agape* love. "We know that we have passed out of death into life, because we love the brothers" (I John 3:14).

Conviction of sin – vv15-17

It is a trustworthy statement that Christ came to save sinners. Paul says I am number one, top of the list, the chief of all sinners. Then he gives a statement of hope by saying that if I can be saved, you certainly can too. Look at my wicked life; God showed grace and mercy towards me. Paul shows his humility. Both James and Peter write that God gives greater grace to the humble. Knowing our sin and that we are sinners causes those who know this to run boldly to the throne of grace.

One week during the spring season I was visiting in my hometown. I walked into a restaurant and happened upon a high school classmate. In fact, he played third base, and I played first on the high school varsity baseball team. In our conversation he asked what I was doing with my life. I told him I was a preacher. He smile, chuckled, and with a huge grin on his face said, "Now tell me what you are really doing." He knew me in my sin. He couldn't grasp my transformation.

Exaltation of the Lord – v18

Paul was a humble believer of praise. Time and again in his writings he inserts a doxology. When God's grace reveals our wretchedness and we discover His forgiveness, we cannot but help praise the Lord. Grace known and realized causes the recipient of mercy to exalt the Lord. The Apostle exalts the Lord with the following descriptions:

- **Kingship:** Eternal or of the ages or king of the ages: Revelation 19:16 supports Paul's doxological expression: "And on His robe and on His thigh He has a name written, "KING OF KINGS, AND LORD OF LORDS.""

- **Immortal** – never to perish, die, nor decay, or be incorruptible: "Jesus Christ is the same yesterday and today and forever" (Hebrews 13:8).
- **Invisible** – only known by His revelation of Himself: We cannot make him appear or be known.
- **Honor and glory forever.** Every follower of Jesus lives a life for His honor and glory.

Like Paul, when I know my sinfulness and know His grace, my response is to thank him, and magnify Him as my Creator. These Psalms express the point:

"O magnify the Lord with me, and let us exalt his name together (34:3). I will praise the name of God with a song. I will magnify him with thanksgiving (69:30). Bless the Lord, O my soul and all that is in me, bless his holy name! Bless the Lord, O my soul and forget not all his benefits" (103:1, 2).

When God is magnified through my gratitude, then He overshadows me. What comes forth is humility. When humility is born, then I am satisfied. I'm no longer on the throne of my life; and I desire to submit. Humility grows in the fertile soil of gratitude. Humility's fruit is submission. Submission equals obedience to the Word. John Piper's theme for his church summarizes this section, "God is most glorified in us when we are most satisfied in Him."[45]

---

45 John Piper, *Seeking and Savoring Jesus Christ*, (Wheaton, Illinois, Crossway Books, 2001), 16.

The evaluation process and expectations of the staff and congregation are critical to the renewal or possibly the survival of a church. The current pastor or transitional pastor along with the called lay leadership must have the courage to restructure their church God's way. Allow the Holy Spirit to lead so that the glory of our Lord will shine brightly in our communities and beyond. The leadership must be exemplary models of grace, humility, and submissiveness. If leaders cannot keep pride off the stage of their hearts, then they cannot expect the congregation to do so either. The members of the congregation must be encouragers. If they live under the umbrella of grace, they will be the staff's cheer leaders. And when equipped to do ministry, they will be so involved and invested in their ministry that they will not have time to cause a ruckus in church.

Here are the expectations used by some churches. Instead of reinventing the wheel, some churches used Rick Warren's church covenant relationship model as described in the *Purpose Driven Church:*[46]

---

[46] Rick Warren, *Purpose Driven Church*, (Grand Rapids, Michigan, Zondervan Publishing House, 1995), 321-322.

(CHURCH NAME) MEMBERSHIP EXPECTATIONS

At (church name) we never ask our members to do more than the Bible clearly teaches. We only expect our members to do what the Bible expects every Christian to do. These responsibilities are spelled out in the Membership Covenant as stated below: Note: (Scripture verses below are from the New American Standard Bible).

I have received Jesus Christ as my Lord and Savior, and I have been baptized by immersion, and I have completed *Discovering Church Name* new member class. From the new member class, I understand and I am in agreement with (church name) *Vision, Mission, Discipleship Process*, and its leadership structure. Thus, I am now led to unite with the (church name) family. In doing so, I commit myself to God, to the other members, and the *Vision (Glorifying Jesus, Growing in Grace, Going by Faith)* and the *Mission (United with Christ to Advance God's Kingdom for His Glory)* by honoring the following:

1. I WILL PROTECT THE UNITY OF MY CHURCH:

- **By acting in love toward other members**
- **By refusing to gossip**
- **By praying for and respecting the ministerial staff**

  - "So then we pursue the things which make for peace and the building up of one another" (Romans 14:19).

- "Now may the God who gives perseverance and encouragement grant you to be of the same mind with one another according to Christ Jesus" (Romans 15:5).
- "Since you have in obedience to the truth purified your souls for a sincere love of the brethren, fervently love one another from the heart" (1 Peter 1:22).
- "Let no unwholesome word proceed from your mouth, but only such a word as is good for edification according to the need of the moment, so that it will give grace to those who hear" (Ephesians 4:29).
- "Obey your leaders and submit to them, for they keep watch over your souls as those who will give an account. Let them do this with joy and not with grief, for this would be unprofitable for you" (Hebrews 13:17).

2. I WILL SHARE THE RESPONSIBILITY OF MY CHURCH

- **By praying for its growth**
- **By inviting the unchurched to attend**
- **By warmly welcoming those who visit**

  - "We give thanks to God always for all of you, making mention of you in our prayers" (1 Thessalonians 1:2).
  - "And the master said to the slave, 'Go out into the highways and along the hedges, and compel them

to come in, so that my house may be filled" (Luke 14:23).

- "Therefore, accept one another, just as Christ also accepted us to the glory of God" (Romans 15:7).

3. I WILL SERVE THE MINISTRY OF MY CHURCH

- **By discovering my gifts and talents**
- **By being equipped to serve by my pastors**
- **By developing a servant's heart**

  - "As each one has received a special gift, employ it in serving one another as good stewards of the manifold grace of God" (1 Peter 4:10).
  - "And He gave some as apostles, and some as prophets, and some as evangelists, and some as pastors and teachers, [12] for the equipping of the saints for the work of service, to the building up of the body of Christ" (Ephesians 4:11-12).
  - "Do nothing from selfishness or empty conceit, but with humility of mind regard one another as more important than yourselves" (Philippians 2:3f).

4. I WILL SUPPORT THE TESTIMONY OF MY CHURCH

- **By attending faithfully at least twice per month barring health, vacation, and other reasonable circumstances**

- **By living a godly life**
- **By giving regularly**

  - "Let us not give up the habit of meeting together... but let us encourage one another" (Hebrews 10:25).
  - "Only conduct yourselves in a manner worthy of the gospel of Christ, so that whether I come and see you or remain absent, I will hear of you that you are standing firm in one spirit, with one mind striving together for the faith of the gospel" (Philippians 1:27).
  - "On the first day of every week each one of you is to put aside and save, as he may prosper, so that no collections be made when I come" (1 Corinthians 16:2).

Conclusion

Having clear expectations of staff and congregation will allow churches to navigate more easily around the icebergs of unforgiveness, Phariseeism, and gracelessness. Evaluation and Biblical expectations are critical in the restoration and health of the church. When expectations are in harmony, relationship building is continuous, and assessments made, the church can maneuver through the next two letters in R.E.S.C.U.E. – streamlined governance and a concise and clear vision and mission.

CHAPTER 3

Leaders are not representatives of a congregation,
but representatives of the kingdom of God.

S.

Streamlined Governance

Except for the family, the church is the greatest God-created institution on the planet. Churches dot the landscape of our globe. In fact, Jesus died for His bride, the church, and He is coming again for His church – His bride. With Jesus as the Creator of the church, how come so many churches have problems? Why do so many church folk argue, fight, and then split? Where is the unity or oneness of the church for which Jesus prayed in His priestly prayer? The problem lies with us; yes, the Christians.

Christians are the problem! Without a doubt we have become the world's excuse for not coming to church. This has been a gradual transition within the church. Over time the church has became more and more self-centered. This began with our buildings. Churches invest more in their buildings than in kingdom advancement. From the 1950's many congregations built the typical rectangular sanctuary with red carpet and white pews. Later, the architectural theme for churches became more modern with state of the art technical capabilities, movie screens, semi-circular seating, and movie theater cushioned chairs.

Presently, church buildings have become almost unidentifiable. They are remodeled hotels, warehouses, or store fronts; however, whatever shape a church has taken, the physical structure of the church has not solved the unity problem. Often physical attributes have caused disunity. At Church C, we built a new sanctuary. A near split almost occurred over the color of the carpet. The church voted for teal carpet over red carpet by only one or two votes. Thank God for that vote! The state of North Carolina didn't need another church with the fifties traditional red carpet. The grapevine chatter was accusatory towards the chairman of the body of deacons and me. People knew I didn't want red. How silly church folk can become! They can work up a lather over nothing. Or my favorite expression: they can get torn out of their frame.

The governance component of churches has not created a oneness in churches. Basically, there are two forms of church governance: congregational and elder models. Simply stated, the congregational model has been in the driver's seat for a fairly long time. In this model the congregation sets the vision and makes decisions. The congregational model is lead by the pastor. The buck stops at his desk.

On the other hand, the single pastor elder or elders of a church give oversight to the body of Christ, and the congregation submits to the vision, direction, and decisions of this church's elected body. Only in matters of calling pastors, purchasing land, approving budgets, bylaw changes, and electing lay leadership does the congregation weigh in on matters.

The predominant Biblical model is the plurality of elders. Elders include the pastor, selected ordained staff, and elected lay male leaders. This group is comprised of the most mature from a congregation. Primarily, this model overrides the congregational form of governance. Why? A congregation has individuals across the spiritual growth spectrum. A church should have its most mature making spiritual decisions to guide the church for God's glory. The *Titanic* was fully booked, but I seriously doubt the passage log would have been filled if folks thought the crew or a few appointed passengers was going to navigate the ship to America. The elders of the church are set apart mainly, because they are called to the office, they can teach, and they are not recent converts (I Timothy 3:1-7). Certainly, the other qualifications of the text are to be considered as well. Now instead of decision making flowing from a member's opinion, desire, or tradition, a decision now comes from the elder body who have an excellent grasp of the Word of God.

Priesthood of the believer or soul competency arguments are the trump cards played to support congregational government. This doctrine, however, simply means a Christian has direct access to the Lord, and he or she does not have to go to priests, pastors, or chaplains for prayers to be delivered to God. This doctrine doesn't mean that all Christians have the maturity level to lead a congregation. In the congregational governance model any member can vote. It doesn't matter that children, inactive members, and, unfortunately, unregenerate members can cast a spiritual decision for a church. A congregational led church complicates the church's ability to move forward spiritually.

Approval of a church matter requires a torturous maze through the deacons and numerous committees. If the pastor desires to move forward in certain areas, he must be a mongrel strain of a little gymnast and a smooth talking salesman. He will have to jump through a number of hoops (committees) to sell his idea. If he convinces the deacons that the idea benefits the church, he has to convince the stewardship, personnel, and even facilities committees. Once they are aligned, step one is complete.

The congregation must now consider the idea. At this point three months have lapsed. The congregation needs to pray as did the deacons and committees, and often a study committee is formed. By God's amazing grace, in six months the idea crystallizes, but the enthusiasm and motivations have waned. *Glacial* (my emphasis) decision making has quenched the Holy Spirit's leadership about the idea.

Pastor, are you tired of being a gymnast-salesman? Most pastors should have a semester's work in sales at a car dealership to learn how to sell the congregation to purchase tangibles. Tangibles are the buildings to be built, playgrounds to be updated, and equipment to be purchased. To achieve congregational approval for the intangibles, like ministry, mission, and administrative ideas, a semester in the New York Life Insurance sales training would be advisable. Life insurance, an intangible, is not realized until a death benefit is paid. A ministry idea is not realized until it is implemented and the fruit from the ministry realized.

What constitutes a church member? As earlier stated, though a person has not attended, contributed financially, or prayed for the church, the majority of churches ironically allow anyone to vote who is on the church roll. Now doesn't this seem odd? The church allows the immature and non-believers to make spiritual decisions for the church. The voting member may cast his vote on emotion, church grapevine chatter, or ill feeling toward a staff person. I do not think that this is what Jesus intended when He gave His life for His church. Again, please, don't trump my thoughts with "the priesthood of the believer" or the "soul competency" argument. Both are true, but my wildcard is spiritual maturity. Spiritual maturity is that part of the equation of our salvation termed sanctification. Many Christians are stunted or have stagnated in their spiritual growth. The attendance and activity in each church I served was approximately forty-five percent of the membership roll. I believe the answer for churches' flourishing is the trustworthy leadership of the called staff and elected elder leadership.

Trust Your Leadership and Leadership be Trustworthy
Calling the Pastor = Trusting the Pastor

Trust Your Leadership

"You have achieved excellence as a leader when people will follow you everywhere if only out of curiosity,"[47] stated Colin Powell. "The true measure of leadership is influence-nothing more, nothing less,"[48] writes John Maxwell. Frank Tillapaugh writes, "Greater the relationships fewer the rules."[49] The church unleashed is built on trust, and trust is built on relationships. The "R" never goes away in the process of renewal and transformation.

Influencing my approach to leadership has been John Maxwell's passionate insights on the topic to Henry Blackaby's heart for a pastor's leadership qualities. The one person in Scripture, however, with whom I identify is Nehemiah. Now he was a leader. People followed him, maybe from curiosity, but more likely from influence. Congregations have to trust their leadership. Ed Young, Jr. of Dallas, Texas started with about one hundred members and now has more than twenty-seven thousand. In an *Executive Magazine* interview he was asked why the church grew, Young answered:

"Around the world I'd have to say in my opinion the biggest hurdle to the church growth and leadership development has to be selfishness. There's no doubt about it. When we can

---

[47] John Maxwell, *21 Irrefutable Laws of Leadership*,(Nashville, Tennessee, Thomas Nelson, Inc., 1998), 11

[48] Ibid.,13.

[49] Frank R. Tillapaugh, *Unleashing the Church*, (Ventura, California, Regal Books, 1982), 77.

unselfishly give up that control and responsibility and then let the leaders lead, then I think the sky is the limit. This may be a radical statement, but I think many church structures are structured for frustration instead of being structured for real success."[50]

Remember submissiveness: not having to be right or in control all the time?

George Barna, the guru of church analysis writes: "the American church is dying due to lack of strong leadership." Henry Blackaby states in *Spiritual Leadership*, "There is nothing more important than leadership." Pastors influence a church body to change for the advancement of personal and corporate spiritual growth. Edward Clowney writes in his book *The Church*; "The officers of the church, who train, assist and encourage the saints who carry out the calling of the church in the world."[51] In other words, leaders train the membership to advance the kingdom of God through their vocations and ministries.

A church calls a lead pastor, who is an elder, but will the church trust their leader? The question arises because of the problem over control or power within the church. Until congregations understand that they cannot lead themselves, churches will not effectively influence their communities. Pastors are called by congregations to plot a course to honor

---

[50]   Ed Young, Jr., *Church Executive Magazine Video*, (Church Executive.com., July 2010).

[51]   Edward P. Clowney, *The Church*, (Downers Grove, Illinois, Intervarsity Press, 1995), 99.

and to glorify the Lord. Pastors and staff are to direct the Body of Christ to be Christ-like by example (I Peter 5:2). God gives called leaders the gift of vision of what the church could and can be to a community. As referenced earlier, Blackaby writes, "Spiritual leadership is leading people on to God's agenda." God's people must trust their called leaders to do that.

I am tickled when I read classified ads of churches seeking pastors. The majority of ads read something like this:

> A senior pastor who is evangelical, homiletically superior and a visionary with a servant's heart, visit the shut-ins, members and prospects, with 10+ years experience, and a heart for people.

They desire to hire a superman saint not a leader to lead. In order to reach the community and the next generation for Christ, the "c" word has to come into play – change. Without change of methodologies churches will cease to influence their communities for Christ. This is where the rub comes for most churches. The old guard says "NO" to change. In one of my churches I removed the doxology from the order of service. On Monday morning I had ten ladies at my study door crying that it was no longer worship for them. In my first church we outgrew our sanctuary, and I wanted to move to a nearby elementary school. Again, church tradition became a show stopper. Recently, changing the governing documents of a church was like running in the Boston Marathon: we did make it up Heartbreak Hill though.

Too many enthusiastic seminarians are graduates with high ideals of how to reach communities only to have a wet blanket thrown over their ideas. I mentioned earlier H.B. London of *Focus on the Family* is a Barnabas to pastors. In one of his conferences he referred to those church members who don't want to change as *joy suckers.* I hate to write the cliché, because it has been stated so often but one more time, "We haven't done it that way before." This statement is the death sentence for so many churches. Churches must trust the pastor not cruelly condemn him.

Leaders Be Trustworthy

On the other side of the leadership coin of trust is the leader. Leaders must be trustworthy. Too many have fallen to sexual misconduct, heavy handed authoritarian leadership style, and financial mismanagement, creating an atmosphere of mistrust. Consequently, the membership seizes the church to operate from fear rather than faith. How can the pastor or eldlers earn the trust of the congregation?

Again, let's look to Nehemiah. First, he was a man of prayer. He wept, fasted, and prayed for the condition of his people. Pastors must pray for those who are critical of him or oppose him. We must weep over their spiritual state. Like Nehemiah we must intercede for them so that God will change their hearts.

Over the years my prayer for members who were at serious odds with me would be threefold: first, that God would transform their hearts, not necessarily to agree with me but at least to respect my direction or decision; second, that they would attend another church; and third that the Lord would take them home. Now I know that is hard, but Nehemiah told his naysayers, "...but you have no portion, right or memorial in Jerusalem" (Nehemiah 2:20).

My more appealing prayer for the congregation, however, is that I pray for at least ten church members per week. My secretary gives me the names, and I download them onto my I-Phone. Prior to the week of my prayer for the ten, the secretary sends a postcard sharing with them that I will be praying for them. The response has been overwhelming. Members have e-mailed, written letters, and telephoned prayer requests to me. I thank my seminary professor and now full time pastor, Stephen Rummage for the idea.

Second, Nehemiah was a man of humility. He indicated that the hand of the Lord was upon him (2:8, 18). James and Peter both write that the humble receive greater grace (James 4:6, I Peter 5:5). The pastor must realize that it is God working through him, and God is allowing him by His grace to succeed in the ministry to which God called him (I Corinthians 15:10). "Not I but Christ" must be riveted to our hearts. As stated earlier, Andrew Murray wrote, "Humility before God is nothing if not proved in humility before men."[52] Intercessory prayer by the pastor for those who persecute the leader is a high-water mark of the leader's humble heart.

---

[52] Andrew Murray, *Humility: The Beauty of Holiness*, (Fort Washington, Pennsylvania, Christian Literature Crusade, 2010), 35.

Third, to gain trust the pastor has to set the example. Nehemiah displayed the model before the people, and they followed him to rebuild the wall. Peter gives a snapshot of the character of the pastor in his first letter (I Peter 5:1-5). Exercise oversight of the flock under your charge. First, understand the grave responsibility pastors have watching over the souls of men (Hebrews 13:17). Eagerly and enthusiastically minister to the people and with the people. Let love for the people, not a pay check, motivate the pastor to lead a church. Exhibit trust in the Lord and walk with the Lord. Be devoted to prayer, to the Word, and to ministry. These actions influence the lives of the church member.

Once, a congregant wrote a letter to the deacons, personnel committee, and church family characterizing me as an authoritarian leader. I gave the letter to our Executive Pastor, and he read it to our leadership, who reaffirmed my call to the church. I had to do two things: pray for my accuser and show grace to him. I have taught both of these biblical principles throughout my ministry. How pastors handle conflicts is what influences the sheep. Reaction to criticism and bad circumstances speak volumes to the bystanders.

During the past twenty years I have continuously had health issues. These health concerns began with two heart attacks at the age of forty-four. In fact, the cardiologist told my wife to gather the family when the second one occurred on the day after the first. During the next ten years I had five heart cauterizations. Then, within an eighteen month period I had both of my retinas detach. A detached retina usually develops a cataract. No, I wasn't an exception. Next, a partial knee replacement, then a stomach hernia and esophageal surgery, followed by eye surgery to remove debris and water from behind one eye and the list could continue with minor illnesses. Jokingly, I say, I've built two wings for hospitals in two different towns. I share this to say that the Lord has used all of these health episodes to help me minister to the congregations. Again, the congregant is watching the pastor to see how he handles his life issues. When the pastor gives glory to the Lord and gratitude in the circumstance, he has preached a sermon the flock won't forget. Oh, yes, just recently I've been diagnosed with "General Neuropathy." And the beat goes on to our Lord's praise, of course.

The community is hearing about your church. They hear the good, the bad, and the ugly stuff that is happening behind the stained glass windows. You are the talk of the town. When the church trusts the pastor, and the pastor is trustworthy, some of the community might come to see what all the excitement is.

The unanswered question that surfaces is who holds the pastor accountable? The scriptures point to a body of elders within the church. These are spiritual men who surround the pastor with prayer, love, and wisdom. A church body calls the pastor and elects its elders to lead it. The pastor is an elder who is the "Lead, teaching elder. Every Christian has the Holy Spirit working in his life. Not every Christian is on the same spiritual playing field so a congregation sets apart spiritually mature men who qualify for the office of elder (I Timothy 3). Then the body calls deacons to serve the congregation (Acts 6,

I Timothy 3). The elders and the deacons set the example of a Christ-like life.

The elders work in concert with the submissive pastor in handing direction, discipline, doctrine, and oversight of the church. On the other hand, deacons support the pastor by performing servant ministries to the membership so that the pastor can focus on praying, preaching, and teaching the Word of God (Acts 6). A deacon body performs hospital, bereavement, homebound, and other ministries the congregation might need. Now the foundation is solid for building a strong church of pilgrims.

The key to the movement of the church's showing authenticity is that the congregation submits to its appointed leadership (Hebrews 13:17). Churches have crumbled under the weight of the congregational vote when they do not follow the elected leadership. Rick Warren in his work, *The Purpose Driven Church*, states that the more voting a church does the more it divides the congregation.[53] How many times have churches divided over issues of little substance? The sin of control raises its ugly head, and the membership fights over the matter. Groups are formed and the loudest most persuasive group usually wins. This is not a godly way to handle church matters. A democratic system more often than not allows the curtain to be opened to show who is on the stage of our sinful nature - pride.

---

[53]   Rick Warren, *Purpose Driven Church: New Member Material*, (Grand Rapids, Michigan, Zondervan Publishing House, 1995), 16.

The question: are congregations mature enough to govern themselves? I would say no! Before e-mailing me a stern letter, hear my rationale for such a statement. All Christians are at different levels in their spiritual growth. It makes no sense to have a child or teen vote on matters in a church. In addition, sad to write, most adult Christians are not in the Word of God daily. Consequently, most churches have immature Christians making decisions for the Body. Decisions are based more on experience, emotion, and church network allegiance than on Scripture.

The graph below demonstrates a simple truth, one that I've experienced in most of the churches I have served. The larger the church, the smaller the decision making body of the church. Only the small church size can try to operate at the congregational level; however, even the smaller churches should follow the single elder model of governance until other spiritually mature men are called to the office. The graph shows how churches should govern themselves:

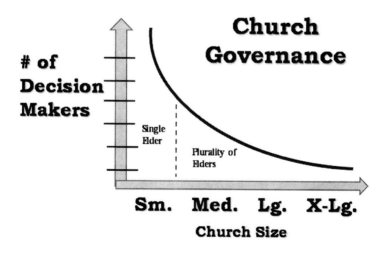

Multiple studies reveal that the number one reason pastors are dismissed, or forced to resign is leadership issues. Churches must decide who will lead them: the congregation or a body of elders which includes the lead pastor or elder. Interestingly enough, throughout Scripture the reader will discover that a congregation or a group of people never led. A survey of the Old Testament shows time and again that God appointed a leader to direct the Israelite nation. In the New Testament, one will discover that Paul instructed the church to "appoint elders" in every church (Acts 14:23, Titus 1:5). Examine the two governance styles below: [54]

Church Governance
Single-Elder Congregationalism

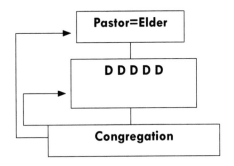

The above diagram shows the congregation electing its officers – elders and deacons.

---

[54] Steven B. Cowan, *Who Runs the Church*, (Grand Rapid, Michigan, Zondervan Publishing House, 2004), 9f

Congregationalism is that form of the church which rests on the independence and autonomy of each local church as defined by the *Oxford Dictionary of the Christian Church.*

1. Rationale for Congregationalism:

    a. Christ is the Head of the Church
    b. Members are priests unto God
    c. The Church is autonomous and operates through a democratic process (Baptist Faith and Message 2000) by the congregation's electing the leadership then following the leadership.

4. Rationale against Congregationalism:

    a. There is an unbalanced spiritual maturity of congregants; some are on "milk" others on "meat." Hebrews 4: I Peter 2:2
    b. There may be unregenerate membership.
    c. It is unwieldy in practice.
    d. In an untested membership the few make decisions for the whole.

5. Terms:

    a. Shepherd – Pastor – Poime
    b. Elder – Ruler – Presbuterous
    c. Bishop – Overseer – Episkopos

    } Terms are interchangeable referring to the same office.

4. Possible Outcome:

    a. **Pastor** becomes the authoritative figure of the church. **Staff** and Pastor are seen as the elders.

    b. **Deacons:** Are they spiritual leaders of the church, or servants to the church, or both? What does the Bible teach?

Apparent Scripture support: (I Cor.5; II Cor.2:6-8 same issue), Matt.18:15-17; Acts 11:22; Acts 13:1-3; Acts 6:1-7; Acts 15:22-23)

Plural-Elder Congregationalism

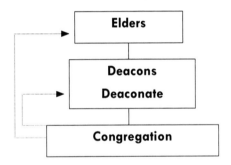

Eldership and deacon are the two offices of the church (Phil. 1:1). The elders oversee the welfare of the church protecting its doctrine, unity, and ministry.

Early Baptist history supports the elders system of governance. W.B. Johnson, first president of SBC, "taught that

Christ strictly required each church to have plural eldership."[55] The Baptist Faith and Message 1925 states, in the church section, that the two church offices are elders and deacons. Even though "elder" was changed to "pastor" in 1963 and 2000 BF&M writings, Herschel Hobbs the lead drafter of the 1963 document states that pastor and elder are the same office.[56]

1. Rationale for Plurality Eldership:

a. Doctrine is guarded: Acts 20:17;27-30
b. Discipline is enforced: Heb.13:17; Matt.18:15f; Gal.6:1-2
c. The true church is one that preaches the Word, observes the ordinances (Communion and Baptism), and practices church discipline.
d. Elders evaluate the progress and health of the church's agreed direction of the vision and mission of the church: I Peter 5:2; I Thess. 5:12-13 "have charge over you" refers to leading and directing the church
e. Elders are examples by modeling the Christian life: I Peter 5:3; I Tim.3:2; Titus 1:6
f. Deacons can focus on ministry to the church: Acts 6:1-7
g. Eldership develops trust between the congregation and leadership: the congregation appoints the leadership and

---

55 Paul A. Newton, *Elders in Congregational Life*, (Grand Rapids, Michigan, Kregel Publications, 2005), 28-29.
56 Herschel H. Hobbs, *What Baptists Believe*, (Broadman Press, 1964) p. 85.

votes on staff, budget, facility expansion, loans, and land purchases; the elders oversee day to day operations

h. There is a diversity of leadership with called staff and elected elders uniting the congregation with leadership.

2. Rationale against Plural Eldership:

a. Total control of the church can rest in an authoritarian leadership
b. There is an elitist group in the church
c. Eldership robs membership of its ability to give direction for the church
d. The staff is supported by, and accountable to, elders. The senior pastor is a part of the elder body.

Apparent Scriptural support: Acts 11:30; 13:1; 14:23; 20:17; Titus 1:5; James 5:14; I Peter 5:1-3; Philippians 1:1

The plurality of elder leadership is an excellent model for protecting a pastor. The pastor submits to the authority of the elders of the church, and together they create a close spiritual bond as they pray, minister, and vision. A pastor must have accountability. Accountability builds trust with the congregation and protects the pastor, as well.

The congregation operates democratically by its calling of the ministerial staff and by electing its elders, deacons, and other lay leaders. Once it has called and elected its leadership; the congregation must submit and trust it to lead.

Earning a Trust Account with the Congregation

The dividend of accountability is trust. When a pastor submits to the eldership of a church, then the congregation can more easily do so. A pastor cannot simply say, "Trust me!" He must earn the trust of the people he is leading. This does not mean that he has to be perfect, but he must have a heart that asks for forgiveness, says, "I'm sorry," when he is wrong, and displays grace and love to the body of Christ.

Too many pastors feel their position automatically demands that people trust him. Trust banks open when a pastor arrives; however, the trust bank is filled over time. The congregation deposits their trust support as they see the pastor's faithfulness. He is faithful...

1. To the inerrancy of scripture (I Timothy 3:16).
2. To expository preaching to feed the flock (Acts 6:2).
3. To a prayerful devotional life and to a humble walk with the Lord (Acts 6:4, Micah 6:8).
4. To shepherding the flock by exercising oversight, being an example, and displaying eagerness (I Peter 5:1-3).
5. To love (I Corinthians 13:1f) the body of Christ, to teach with patience (II Timothy 4:2), and to watch over its souls (Hebrews 13:17).

As the pastor fulfills these Scriptural mandates, his trust account grows. As he walks in love, in the light, and in the fullness of the Spirit will he be able to be faithful to His call

(Eph.4). Fulfillment of each leadership responsibility earns an increase in the trust account. Below are several examples of the various leadership responsibilities:

Mark Dever illustrates a pastor's leadership with four triangles and circles at top point of the triangle around the acrostic b.o.s.s.:[57]

B - A pastor is called to be the visionary teaching leader. The pastor teaches or instructs through his preaching and teaching. The triangle is upright.

O – The pastor is the example setter in love, forgiveness, and direction. He says, "Come follow me!" The triangle is pointed to the right.

S – The pastor is the supplier for the flock. As a supplier the pastor equips the saints for ministry, encourages them in their walk, and trains others to be the teachers and leaders of tomorrow. The triangle is to the left.

S – The pastor is the servant-leader of the congregation. As one of the overseers, the pastor serves through his faithful teaching, praying, correcting, and exhorting the members under his charge. The triangle is inverted.

---

[57] Mark Dever, *9 Marks of a Healthy Church*, (Wheaton, Illinois Crossway Books, 2004), 236-240.

I expanded Dever's model of leadership to explain the pastor's leadership responsibilities as elder:

Congregation   Leader: Pastor-Elder   Holy Spirit
                                                 Leadership

E – Equips the
    saints for
    ministry
    Ephesians
    4:12

E – Expounds the
    vision for the
    church, Leads,
    and says:
    "Follow me!" I
    Timothy 3:15

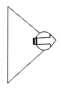

L – Leadership
    through
    Servanthood
    Mark 10:43;
    Romans 1:1

R – Reflects
    Christ's
    character I
    Timothy 4:12

D – Dedicated
    preacher/
    teacher
    of God's
    Word giving
    oversight to
    the church II
    Timothy 4:1-
    4; I Peter 5:2

Warning to pastors: Satan strives to devour, defeat, and depress you. He will do anything to tempt you so that you will fall and fail. He will use people in your congregation to bring you down. The devil and his cohorts have placed a target on your back. Beware! One "Far Side" cartoon has two bucks with huge racks on their heads. One of the bucks has a bull's eye on the shoulder area. The other buck is staring at him, and the caption reads: "Bummer birthmark, Hal." Every pastor has a bull's eye on his back.

Seriously, guard your life closely. Satan, the world, and your flesh are the bullets or arrows aiming at your birthmark. This is why pastors need elders. They can ask the hard questions:

- How are you treating your wife?
- How are you handling your money?
- Describe your prayer and devotional life?
- Do you have sexual desires outside of your marriage?
- Are you looking at pornography or making inappropriate advances or comments to parishioners?
- With what sins are you struggling daily, monthly, or during the year?

A pastor friend tells the story of how he became involved sexually with his children's ministry director. He had feelings towards her but never expressed them. The two of them flirted, but nothing came of the flirtations. After several years of these flirtations the children's ministry director broke down and told the pastor she loved him. Well, the pastor immediately responded that he loved her as well. He went behind her desk, she stood, and they kissed. For months it was kissing in the empty classrooms during the day and before they left for their respective homes. Then one rainy day she invited him "to sleep" with her. For the next eight months they had numerous rendezvous' in hotels. By God's grace the affair ended, and both repented of their sin.

The lesson is that a thought turned into words, and the words turned into action. Stop! Examine the equation: Thought + Words = Action. The late basketball coach of UCLA, John Wooten, told his players, "Your ability got you here; your character will keep you here."[58] So it is with pastors as well. Many pastors have fallen from the ranks because of immoral activity or because of trying to lead in an authoritarian way. James gave the warning:

"Let no one say when he is tempted, "I am being tempted by God"; for God cannot be tempted by evil, and He Himself does not tempt anyone. [14] But each one is tempted when he is carried away and enticed by his own lust." (1:13-14).

Jesus stated that our words reveal the heart; "But the things that proceed out of the mouth come from the heart, and those defile the man." (Matthew 15:18). The desires of the pastor and the children's director were conceived with their words. Words are the parents of desire.

---

[58] John Wooten: http://www.goodreads.com/author/quotes/23041. John_Wooden?page=4

Oh, fellow pastors and elders, guard your hearts from sexual misconduct, authoritarian leadership, and financial irresponsibility! Pastors submit to the Word, the elders over you, and, of course the Lordship of Christ to protect your walk and ministry. Then watch your stock market of trust soar!

Conclusion

A streamlined governance model is critical to church growth and unity. Everybody cannot be in charge. Like it or not, everybody is under somebody's authority. The mindset of some church members, however, is that they be captain of the church ship. Glacial decision making is no longer acceptable in our technological culture. Yes, we must pray and seek the Lord's guidance. The pace may quicken as the elder body grapples with decisions to bring to the church, but at least the decision makers are a small biblically driven group of men, not a congregation of hundreds. The reality is that only a handful comes to a church ministry conference or business meeting. Usually, ten percent or less of the congregation attend. This is another reason why the church needs elders to direct the vision and mission, to discipline folks who are out of step with the Lord to reunite them with Lord, and the church; and to keep the doctrine of the church commitment with the church covenant. Finally, elders are to encourage, to protect, and to hold accountable the pastor and staff. Beloved, the congregation cannot lead itself.

Bob Dylan, one of my favorite singers in the 1960's, wrote the lyrics to the song, *Gotta Serve Somebody*. Although he won a Grammy Award for the song, some song critics reviewed the song as his second worst. Despite the mixed opinions about the song, the chorus rings a Biblical truth: whom will we serve: God or Satan? We might respond by saying we will serve ourselves. This is simply another reply indicating allegiance to Satan. The Devil's desire is to destroy the church. When church members do not follow church leaders, the church runs aground. Americans serve their country by obeying the laws and paying their taxes. Christians serve their church by making decisions to advance God's kingdom in an orderly, expediently, and godly manner. Satan loves church! He loves it when churches fight, and members become the authority, so that he gains a strong foothold. Dylan is right. You are going to serve somebody. Will we serve to advance our kingdoms or the kingdom of God?

CHAPTER 4

Concise and clear Biblically originated vision and mission statements are the church's compass.

C.

Concise and clear vision and mission statements with a discipleship process are necessary to grow and train believers to advance the kingdom of God.

Another Atlantic Ocean tragedy occurred on July 16, 1999. John F. Kennedy, Jr., crashed his Piper aircraft into the open waters of the Atlantic. Wikipedia records that numerous factors contributed to this avoidable disaster, and Kennedy; his wife, Carolyn Bessette, and her sister, Lauren Bessette, did not have to perish in the water. Let's examine a few of the contributing factors to the crash that parallel pastor and church heartaches. Evaluators of the crashed plane determined ten influences that contributed to the accident:

1. **Haze and visibility:** The evening sky was hazy; and visibility was poor, creating an atmosphere where spatial disorientation could occur. Defined by Wikipedia, *Spatial disorientation is the inability to correctly interpret aircraft attitude, altitude or*

airspeed, in relation to the Earth or point of reference, especially after a reference point (e.g., the horizon) has been lost. Spatial disorientation is a condition in which an aircraft pilot's perception of direction does not agree with reality.

Evidently, the crash occurred when Kennedy flew into this challenging environment causing him to lose his focus.

2. Pilot inexperience

3. **Pilot training** – Kennedy qualified to fly in good night conditions with the instrument panel. His instructor, however, stated that he was not ready to fly in poor weather conditions.

4. Psychological stress

5. **Pilot distraction** – When departing from the New Jersey airport, Kennedy nearly struck another plane. The incident was described as "most uncomfortable."

6. **No flight plan or request for help** – Technically, no flight plan was required for this flight, but no one knew Kennedy's flight path to Martha's Vineyard. In addition, when the plane was in trouble, Kennedy never radioed for assistance.

7. Late departure

8. **Flight over featureless, open water** – The Aircraft Handbook clearly states that flying over large bodies of water at night is dangerous. The horizon blends with the water, making orientation and perception difficult.

9. Injured foot

10. **Wrong frequencies** – After recovering the wreckage, the investigators found that both of Kennedy's radios were dialed into the wrong frequencies. This may not have contributed to the crash, but it could have thwarted his signal for help.

Now let's take six of the ten possible causes of Kennedy's plane crash and compare them to a church's spinning out of control towards its demise.

1. The church's haze and visibility. Many a church loses it focus or has no vision or mission plan causing a fog to develop around the church. Thus, the current reality of the church is not understood. In one church I served, the leadership thought that the problem was its current staff. The reality was not the staff but the church school. The school was the haze in which the church was flying causing the church to become disoriented. As stated earlier, traditions, idols, pharisaical ideas, and behaviors cloud ministry visibility.

2. The church's lack of leadership parallels Kennedy's lack of training. It amazes me that so many lay folk think they can lead a church better than trained, educated, and experienced staff. A church-led church will stymie its grow and potential. Conversely, it amazes me when pastors lead a church away from Biblical standards.

Seminaries must train pastors better in conflict management and teach them leadership skills. The truth in any organization is that when there is a leadership vacuum someone or some group will fill the vacancy. The deacons in a church I served did not lead. Prior to my coming, they allowed the majority of a Sunday School class to fill the vacuum indirectly. The class leaders created turmoil against the staff which overflowed into a church business meeting. In short, the church crucified the staff and lost its bearings.

To prevent a drought of leadership in a church, the church should have a discipleship process to assist believers to grow in their faith by walking together in order to learn from each other. Discipleship is an integral part of the R in R.E.S.C.U.E. – Relationships. In three of the churches I served, the process was gather, connect, train, and go. We gather for worship, connect in our small groups (Sunday School or home groups), train through classes and accountability relationships, and go in our ministry and mission endeavors. In this discipleship process leaders will surface, and they will be leaders who lead from a biblical perspective.

3. Pilot distraction mirrors church distractions. Churches become distracted by focusing on the insignificant and "make mountains out of mole hills." Methodology is a huge distraction within many churches. Methodologies create change. Change is difficult for many. My favorite cartoon is the one in which the preacher is being led to the gallows to be hung. The line under the caption reads: "I told him not to change the order of service."

Vision and mission statements are not what grow believers or a church, but give direction and a reminder of what the church is. As these statements are formulated, they must be birthed from Scripture. Too many times churches will use a catchy phrase which has no Biblical undergirding. An unwillingness to change distracts congregants and makes them feel uncomfortable. Consequently, they are distracted from the true purpose of the church and their involvement within the body.

4. No flight plan and no call for help is seen in churches as well. A church's flight plan is its vision and mission. Vision statements are simply about personal growth and church direction. Below is a sample:

    a. Glorifying Jesus (I Cor. 10:31, Jn.16:14),

    b. Growing in Grace (I Cor. 15:10, Rm.5:20, Acts 20:24),

    c. Going by Faith (Heb.11:6)

Mission statements indicate how the church will fulfill its vision. An example which guides the fulfillment of the above vision statement from a church is: "United with Christ to Advance God's Kingdom for His Glory." The statement reminds the believer of his:

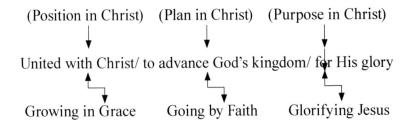

The church's Aviation Handbook is the Bible. The vision and mission statements flow from the Word of God, not from a catchy manmade phrase. The Bible creates the church's flight plan to give the body of believers clear direction.

Please, understand these statements will not enhance the believer or the church as a whole unless there is a strong discipleship process. The statements are mere markers to keep the church on a path of righteousness for the glory of Jesus. They can become excellent evaluation tools as well. The leadership can ask the hard questions of why it is not fulfilling its vision and mission.

In examining the attendance records of a church, I found that it had a ten year decline in attendance, but no one asked the question, "Why?" The church had no vision or mission statement to help evaluate its situation. Sadly, the church came so close to becoming one of the hundreds of churches that cease to exist each year. To its credit the church called for help and now has a focus through its new vision and mission statements and discipleship process. Currently the church has righted itself from the tail spin and is slowly gaining altitude.

5. Flying over featureless bodies of water can be compared to churches' not adhering to Biblical leadership principles. When aircraft fly at night over large bodies of water, the horizon and water seem to appear as one. When a church chooses man's systems over biblical ones, the church is like the aircraft flying over large bodies of water at night. Man's system meets the worldview of life which causes the church to be guided towards disaster.

Man's system consists of churches that are run by committee and not by Scripture. In my last church before retiring, the church had forty-two committees. Each committee was an authority. As cited earlier, the staff spent more time as salesmen than as ministers. Staff had to sell an idea to the deacons; then convince the church council, then a committee or two, then stewardship for funding, and finally to a business meeting for approval. Again, are you exhausted? Believe me, I was! Many good ideas became lost in the red tape mire. In fact, enthusiasm waned after the debates over an idea. One prospect for this church stated to me at an exercise center that if he ran his business like the church, he would have to close his doors very soon. Most churches have glacial movement in making decisions.

Also, hearing so many opinions and suggestions is like flying over a large body of water at night. There are no lights or markers to guide the thoughts and opinions. Too many church organizational systems are flawed. At this particular church the structure was like the United States government. Bottom line: who is in control? Too many chiefs and not enough ministers. Another drawback in most churches is that they teach that ministry is being on a committee. Let's get Mr. Johnny, the new member, to get involved by serving on this committee. Instead of teaching Mr. Johnny to be fulfilled by exercising his spiritual gifts to meet someone's need.

6. Wrong frequencies were found on Kennedy's radios. The report stated that both radios were set incorrectly. The church has two communication systems to keep it on track: the Holy Spirit and the Bible, and they work in concert. It should not surprise us that so many churches are struggling. Arguably, the root cause is poor communication. Even if Kennedy tried to call for help, in his disorientated state he could not reset his frequencies to receive assistance. When leaders and members operate from the flesh, the Holy Spirit is quenched (I Thess. 5:19). The quenching grieves the Holy Spirit (Eph. 5:30) which is His emotional response from being quenched. The Person of the Holy Spirit gives us the advantage in life (John 16:7) so the Christian can glorify Jesus (John 16:14). Depending upon the translation, the Paraclete is described differently. Using one's hand can assist in the remembrance of His work in our lives:

a. Thumb: "Helper" – English Standard Version, New American Standard, King James
   He empowers the believer in his walk.

b. Index finger: "Advocate" – New Living Translation, New International Version
   He pleads our case of innocence and prays for us.

c. Middle finger: "Counselor" – Holman, Revised Standard Version
   He is our teacher and guide working in concert with the Word.

d. Ring finger: "Comforter"– Living Bible
   He is our wonderful most compassionate encourager.

e. Little finger: "Sealer" – English Standard Version
   He seals our salvation; He is our guarantee.

Remembering these characteristics of the Holy Spirit makes Him our "Friend," which is how the Message Bible describes Him.

The other primary source of communication is the Bible. Our Teacher has taken residence in the person of faith in Jesus. He is alive to teach the living Word. Both the Spirit and the Word are life forms in the life of faith. Miserablely, though, most Christians operate from the flesh instead of the Spirit. The Spirit will draw us to the Word, whereas the flesh leads us to the world. The Apostle Paul taught clearly not to be misled by the philosophies of the world (Colossians 2:8). Our way is a way of pride and glory to express our success. Those who operate from this launching point do not understand their sin. The greater one's understanding of sin the greater his dependency on God. When Jesus taught from the mount (Matthew 5), He started by showing our need to understand our spiritual bankruptcy. Examine *Grace Mountain* below to see how God's grace changes us, and how we are to give grace because of our transformation. Understanding the Sermon on the Mount sets the frequency for the Holy Spirit and the Word to be heard.

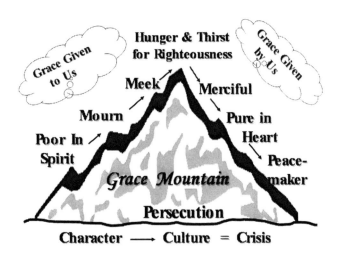

Poor in Spirit is one's spiritual bankruptcy. The diagrams below best describe one's pre and post Christian conditions:

Pre:

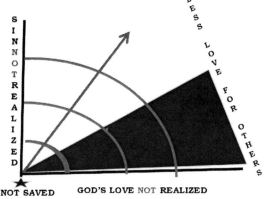

- Enslaved by sin - John.8:34
- Governed by sin - Ephesians 2:3
- Spiritually dead - Ephesians 2:1
- Defiled conscience - Titus 1:15
- Without desire for God – Romans 3:11
- Hostile towards God - Romans .8:7

Post:

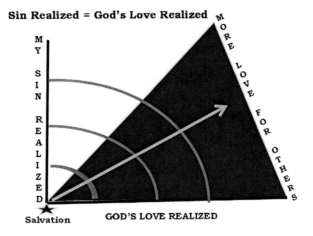

- Holy and blameless - Ephesians - 1:4
- Walking in a manner worthy of the calling with which you have been called - Ephesians 4:1
- Walk in newness of your mind - Ephesians 4:17f
- Walking in love - Ephesians 5:2
- Walking in the Spirit – Galatians 5:25

Conclusion

A church's concise and clear vision and mission are vital to a church's moving forward. They are markers to help evaluate the church's progress in advancing the kingdom of God. The above diagrams force a church to check its vision and mission statements. Is the church maturing believers? Is the church exhibiting grace towards one another and others outside the church? Is the church advancing the kingdom of God? Concise and clear vision and mission statements keep the church on its biblically mandated course. Too many churches have wandered off course. They are the ones A.W.Tozer describes as rotting. However, a church's Biblical vision and mission statement are the compass points that keep a church from going into a tailspin. Make each clear, concise, and Biblical.

CHAPTER 5

The church's greatest evangelistic
methodology is the church's unity.

U.

Unity in the body

"I do not ask on behalf of these alone, but for those also who believe in Me through their word; that they may all be one; even as You, Father, *are* in Me and I in You, that they also may be in Us, so that the world may believe that You sent Me. The glory which You have given Me I have given to them, that they may be one, just as We are one" (John 17:20-22).

Larry Osborne in his book the *Unity Factor* expresses three areas where the church leadership and congregation need, to be singing from the same song sheet.[59]

1. Doctrinally – same belief system around doctrines of the Bible

---

[59] Larry W. Osborne, The Unity Factor, (Vista, California, Owls Nest Publisher, 2006), 10.

2. Philosophically – same belief in vision and mission of the church
3. Relationally – same belief in loving, encouraging, and disciplining the body

If the leadership is not unified, one cannot expect the church to be unified. As go the elders or deacons (depending on your governance model), so goes the church.[60] Here is the most critical statement in Osborne's book, **"Without unity it is virtually impossible to sustain spiritual growth."**[61] (Emphasis added). Unity is the foremost evangelistic methodology in reaching a lost community. Without unity most people will not stay at a church, and others will not invite anyone to the church. Unity builds momentum for a church and creates an atmosphere of excitement and anticipation. Jesus prayed prior to His execution that we would be one so the world would know that He has come. The church's oneness produces glorious prasie to our Lord. If we are not one, then the church's poor testimony only adds to the darkness of the world.

Church business meetings can be sources for breeding disunity. Many churches have either quarterly or monthly meetings (God help them!) To remove some of the sting of business meetings, I renamed them *Ministry Conferences*. As a body of believers we are called together mainly to discuss the ministries of the church. Business principles are applied in

---

[60]   Ibid. 14.
[61]   Ibid.14.

churches, but they are not the driving force of a church. When a church is healthy, finances will not be an ongoing issue, and members come together to discuss the ministries that are supporting the fulfillment of its vision and mission. We only need to have conferences twice a year. The Fall conference is designed to elect the lay leadership approve the budget for the next year, and handle any other ministry agenda item. The Spring Conference is designed to review the previous year and to hear reports from appointed officers and committees. Additional Ministry Conferences may be called at the direction of the leadership.

Between the Ministry Conferences the church has two *Ministry Rallies*. The Ministry Rally was implemented to share progress and future ministries, events, and activities for the upcoming months. Usually there is a meal associated with the rallies along with homemade ice cream. I almost forgot, no business is brought to the floor during these rallies. Each of these rallies is intentionally designed to create greater harmony within the Body.

Woes from Church Voting

A friend was a candidate for a senior pastor position at a Virginia church. Several members created a coup of naysayers against him, and, in fact, one family drove from North Carolina to vote against this pastor.

In one church I served, the deacons approved the installation of a gym floor, but at the subsequent business meeting one disaffected deacon rallied a few other deacons to change their position and encourage the congregation not to install the floor. The political church games we play cause indigestion for many church members and those in the church's community. The grapevine chatter prepares many for the business meeting on how to vote. People are scrambling to persuade individuals from other ministries to come to the meeting to constitute a quorum. When I was a deacon years ago, the pastor asked me to get the nursery workers to attend for the quorum count. After the count they returned with babies in hand to the nursery. Now, that is a funny but sad commentary on church business meetings. But if there is an issue that could cause a fight, then those whom you saw at the last Christmas candle light service are there to vote. What does the Lord think about most church business meetings? Not much I'm sure! I say, let's have fewer votes on issues. Again, to reiterate and to highlight, the more a church votes, the more it divides itself writes Rick Warren.[62] Here are a few areas that need a congregational voice:

1. Calling of staff
2. Election of lay leadership
3. Land purchase or sale
4. Annual budget

---

[62] Rick Warren, *Purpose Driven Church: New Member Material*, (Grand Rapids, Michigan, Zondervan Publishing House, 1995), 16.

5. Borrowing money
6. Bylaw change
7. Any issue the elders or pastor deem necessary to bring to congregation

In the unity book of the Bible (Ephesians 4:1-17), the Apostle Paul has a predicable writing style. He begins with doctrine, inserts a doxology, and then concludes with the delightful duty or application of how to walk by faith. Ephesians, for example, has the first three chapters of doctrine. Chapter Three is highlighted by a beautiful doxology (Ephesians 3:20-21). The last three chapters deal with the believers' walk with the Lord. Paul begins his application by exhorting the believer to walk in a manner worthy of his calling (4:1). *Worthy* means to balance the believer's doctrine with his walk.[63] One falls from the doctrinal balance beam when Pharisaical attitudes of legalism are developed, such as the unwritten law of the dress code for worship: only dresses for women and a tie for men. One stumbles off the other side of the doctrinal balance beam when emotionalism overshadows doctrine. When a family member announces his homosexual lifestyle, does the family respond by renouncing the Biblical position of this sexual sin? In Ephesians 4 Paul delineates walking in a manner worthy of a believer's calling by:

---

[63] Marty Lloyd-Jones, *Ephesians Commentary 4:1-16: Christian Unity*, (Grand Rapids, Michigan, Baker Books, 1980), 24-26.

1. Humility,
2. Gentleness,
3. Patience,
4. Bearing with one another in love,
5. Eagerly maintaining the unity of the Spirit in the bond of peace,
6. Equipping the saints for the work of ministry,
7. Encouraging the body of Christ, until it attains the unity of faith and knowledge of the Son of God;
8. Maturing manhood to the measure of the stature of the fullness of Christ,
9. Not being tossed or carried away by every wind of doctrine;
10. Avoiding human cunnings, and craftiness in deceitful schemes,
11. Speaking truth in love,
12. Growing into Christ,
13. Knowing that Christ holds the church together,
14. Each member's working in his proper place,

As a result the body grows and builds itself in love.

Paul next, as recorded in 4:18-32, lists additional characteristics of a unified body. He begins chapter five by exhorting the believer to walk in love and walk as children of light. He concludes the first section of chapter five by urging the reader to walk wisely, because the days are evil. In other words, a follower of Christ should be worthy of his calling as a believer, a walk in love, light, and wisdom.

Unity is tied to the congregation's submission and the pastor's trustworthiness. A church grows around its oneness for the audience of One, Jesus. One will observe unity in the church when there is ongoing restoration/reconciliation; when evaluations and expectations are achieved; when an agreement on streamlined governance is in place; and when the church has rallied around a vision and mission statement. Notice that the *U* in R.E.S.C.*U*. E. is the foundation for the first four letters in the word. The idea of unity is only wishful thinking, unless the previous letters are fulfilled or being developed. Once unity is established, evangelism can occur.

Conclusion

The verses Jesus prayed in His priestly prayer from the New Living Translation:

> [20] *"I am praying not only for these disciples but also for all who will ever believe in me through their message.* [21] *I pray that they will all be **one**, just as you and I are **one**—as you are in me, Father, and I am in you. And may they be in us so that the world will believe you sent me.* [22] *"I have given them the glory you gave me, so they may be **one** as we are **one**.* [23] *I am in them and you are in me. **May they experience such perfect unity** that the world will know that you*

sent me and that you love them as much as you love me.

When Lee and I were on sabbatical to the Potter's Inn (www. pottersinn.com) in the Rockies, I fell in love with the Aspen tree. Its light colored bark dotted with black spots beautify the Rocky Mountain area and other cold to cool climate regions. An interesting fact about the tree is its root system. Even though Aspens stand independently tall (50feet-100feet), their root systems interlock. This interlocking strengthens the trees and enables them to withstand strong winds and snow storms. Aspens are termed "clonal colony" trees, because the root system of one tree reproduces itself numerous times.

Likewise, the church's root system interlocks the membership in its faith in the Lord and love for one another. Also, like the Aspen tree, the church membership is called to reproduce itself. We are to make disciples. One tree may have other trees sprout from its root system 98 to 138 feet from the parent tree. Each person learning and implementing the discipleship process will create other disciples who may go to other lands with the gospel.

Why the concern for being one? Jesus prayed for unity; Paul wrote about unity; and the early church demonstrated unity (Acts 2:42f). Again, why? So unbelievers would believe. Unity in a church draws others to the church. Unity creates an atmosphere of excitement, anticipation, and enthusiasm. A unified church gains momentum.

Have you ever ridden on a roller coaster? I remember in my younger days enjoying the thrill of this amusement park ride. The ride starts with a steep incline. It chugs and strains on the upward track. In fact, you wonder if it will make it to the top. Then suddenly the first car vanishes before your eyes and then abruptly your car zooms downward as well. Presently, members need to start straining and chugging upward together. Then before long, they will make it over the top interlocked together with great momentum. What a ride they will have together for the glory of our Lord! Eventually, the watching world will want to ride with them as well.

The primary expectation for members is to protect the church's unity. Causing disunity is Satan's scheme to dishonor and destroy the church. Paul's warning in chapter six of Ephesians is to *stand firm* against the schemes of the Devil. *Stand firm* has the meaning of a goal line stance in a football game. In other words, the church is not going to surrender holy ground. In high school our football team had a fifty-one plus game winning streak. The winning streak was in jeopardy during my senior year. The opposition had the ball on the one yard line, first and goal. They ran the ball four times; we stopped them four times short of the goal line. Then our offense drove the ball 99 yards for the winning touchdown. This is the idea behind Ephesians 6:10. Once the church successfully defends holy ground the schemes of the devil cannot score.

Remember, unity is the gauge to watch closely. On this gauge are relationships, expectations, governance, vision, and mission. If the church is not grounded in each of these, then disunity has come knocking on the church's front door. The U. is stabilized when the first four letters are practiced. Without unity the church will be unable to achieve the last letter in the acrostic R.E.S.C.U.E., E.: evangelism. The U. is the doorway for advancing the kingdom of God.

CHAPTER 6

The Christian without a missionary heart is an anomaly.[64]

America is only as beautiful as the church is faithful in advancing God's Kingdom.

E.

Evangelism through a life, Ministry, and Mission

How many evangelism methods have you studied in your Christian walk? I have experienced *Evangelism Explosion, Sharing Your Faith without Fear, Tract Evangelism,* and *F.A.I.T.H.* Each is worthy of studying but each has lived its shelf-life. The downside of each is the end result of the presentations – praying the sinner's prayer. I have witnessed genuine transformations of someone who prayed this prayer. On the other hand, I have observed too many who prayed the prayer without a transformation. How many actually have been born again throughout the years from a Billy Graham Crusade? Like many other pastors I've been guilty of creating an environment of easy believism. Here is the common

---

[64] Colin Marshall and Tony Payne, *The Trellis and the Vine,* (Kingsford, Australia, Matthias Media,.2009), 52.

prescription to encourage, or manipulate, someone to come forward at the end of a worship service: Sing *Just as I Am*, have deacons set the example by coming forward to make the walk more comfortable; and use guilt language (*You may die this afternoon. Are you ready?*; *This may be your last chance*; *aren't you tired of living this way?*; *Jesus died for you, Now what are you going to do for Him?*, or the proof text from Matthew 10:32-33, *Therefore everyone who confesses Me before men, I will also confess him before My Father who is in heaven. But whoever denies Me before men, I will also deny him before My Father who is in heaven.* This text has been used as a punch line to persuade folks to come down and be saved. The text means to speak and display Jesus daily. A last desperate ploy is to sing *Just as I Am* until someone finally comes forward. One version of the well-worn joke is about the man who came forward only to tell the pastor that he has come so we can go home to watch the ball game or so we can go to lunch. Disheartening as this sounds, so many church members evaluate the sermon's impact on how many come forward.

I have this invitation prescription written into the service too many times over three decades. As stated, some truly were transformed, but some are still dripping dry somewhere with a false hope of their salvation. But why do pastors and members gauge the service's success or effectiveness on the number who come forward?

I believe that for too many decades we were taught incorrectly either through seminary or by our older pastor peers that numbers equate success. The majority of churches have only half or less active of their rolls. The good news is that this is changing. Established churches and church plants are doing evangelism differently to assimilate new believers better into the Body of Christ. I believe many are realizing the character of evangelism. It is not simply having someone to say a sinner's prayer; but it is to model the love of Jesus and share the good news as one goes in his life. Examine the following evangelistic characteristics:

I. Evangelism's motivation – To worship God!

Everyone's success derives from motivation. An unmotivated person will not accomplish his goals. Having played sports actively from seven years of age through my twenties, I heard many motivational speeches from coaches. I remember playing basketball against Ohio University. We were the "favorite" to lose the game; and we did by fifty or so points. It was too long ago to remember the exact score, plus, I don't want to remember. The coach before the game said, "Men we put our pants on the same way as they do, one leg at time." What he didn't tell us was that their pant legs were six inches longer than ours!

My primary motivation in track (hurdles), baseball (playing first base, and pitching), or basketball, was to please the coach. I remember in college making a layup on a fast break. After the basket I didn't break stride in running past our bench in front of the coach to hear him say, "Way to hustle, Sadler!"

As Christians, our motivation to evangelize others is so that they can enjoy Jesus as we do. It is through our worship that we engage intimately with Him. Whether through our alone time or corporate time with Jesus, we bow before Jesus to give Him praise. John Piper slam dunks the idea:

> *The most crucial issue in missions is the centrality of God in the life of the church. How can people who are not stunned by the greatness of God be sent with the ringing message, "Great is the Lord, and great to be praised; he is to be feared above all gods" (Psa.96:4). The truth, more than any other I know, seals the conviction that worship is the fuel and goal of missions. The deepest reason why our passion for God should fuel missions is that God's passion for God fuels missions. Missions is the overflow of our delight in God because missions is the overflow of God's delight in being God. And the deepest reason why worship is the goal in missions is that worship is God's goal.*[65]

Christianity is a relationship with Jesus. Mission's motivation is to display our relationship with Jesus because we are so delighted in our union with Him. Jesus saw our need for

---

[65]   John Piper, *Let the Nations Be Glad,* (Grand Rapids, Michigan, Baker Publishing Group,.2010), 38.

forgiveness of sin, and He came to redeem us. He did not see a problem; He saw a person in need. Do we see people, or do we see people as problems?

II. Evangelism's mandate – Go!

The church's view of others is a major factor in its attitude towards fulfilling the mandate to go. If the church only sees problems, then it will develop a fortress mentality. It will hunker down, never seeing the crowd of people in need of Jesus. When our Lord said, "Go", he means, "As you go." As we go, you and I are to acknowledge Him before others so that He will acknowledge us before the Father who is in Heaven (Matthew 10:32). Each gospel author describes Jesus' evangelism directive differently. Bolded words highlight their differences:

> Matthew 28:18-20: "All authority has been given to Me in heaven and on earth. [19] **Go therefore and make disciples** of all the nations, baptizing them in the name of the Father and the Son and the Holy Spirit, [20] teaching them to observe all that I commanded you; and lo, I am with you always, even to the end of the age."

> Mark 16:15: And He said to them, "**Go** into all the world and **preach the gospel** to all creation.

Luke 24:46-49 "and He said to them, "Thus it is written, that the Christ would suffer and rise again from the dead the third day, [47] and that repentance for forgiveness of sins would be proclaimed in His name to all the nations, beginning from Jerusalem. [48] You are witnesses of these things. [49] And behold, I am sending forth the promise of My Father upon you; but you are to stay in the city until you are **clothed with power from on high**."

John 21:18-22: Truly, truly, I say to you, when you were younger, you used to gird yourself and walk wherever you wished; but when you grow old, you will stretch out your hands and someone else will gird you, and bring you where you do not wish to *go*." [19] Now this He said, signifying by what kind of death he would glorify God. And when He had spoken this, He *said to him, **"Follow Me!"**[20] Peter, turning around, *saw the disciple whom Jesus loved following *them*; the one who also had leaned back on His bosom at the supper and said, "Lord, who is the one who betrays You?" [21] So Peter seeing him *said to Jesus, "Lord, and what about this man?" [22] Jesus *said to him, "If I want him to remain until I come, what *is that* to you? **You follow Me!"**

Jesus' last words were for Christians to "go," to "preach," and to "follow" Him. We are to follow Jesus by going into all nations to make disciples by proclaiming the forgiveness of sins. Churches that are going beyond their walls are fulfilling the mandate given by our Lord. Churches with no mission heart are indeed an abnormality. How can church members overcome this abnormality?

1. Pray for an evangelistic heart for their church and for themselves: Christians need to be Holy Spirit sensitive. In one's morning devotional, or quiet time, or drive to work, pray that the Lord would present an opportunity to share Him. Giving a cup of cold water, money, clothes, or the gospel message is our primary daily task.

2. Give to evangelistic endeavors: Cooperative Program of Southern Baptist churches or whatever similar denominational structure one's church undertakes. Most denominations have a giving structure to support missionaries and other evangelistic ministries.

3. Support a church plant by a local church.

4. Manifest evangelism through the fruit of the Spirit.

Unless an individual active in ministry manifests the fruit of the Spirit, his ministry is meaningless and useless. Too many pastors and lay ministers cloud the exercise of their God given gifts by the lack of love, joy, peace, or one of the other six fruits. Evangelism is a vehicle that carries the character of Jesus into our individual relationship networks and beyond. The Spirit's fruit magnifies one's ministry. People see the giver's love more than the giver's offering. I've heard feedback from numerous people who have been helped as to how nice, loving, kind, or pleasant the giver was to them, not what the individual did for them. If one cannot display the fruit, he makes his service gift invisible, because he did not represent the kingdom of God correctly. Imagine giving a cup of water without compassion? Imagine dispensing food from the church's food closet without genuine concern for the person. Imagine being demanding to the waiter in the restaurant, unkind to the nurse caring for a relative in the hospital, or being impolite or cold towards a visitor at your church. Let me ask, how ripe is the fruit of the Spirit? I love apples. Occasionally, though, I have bitten into an apple that was bruised. My facial expression changes, and I quickly spit it out (of course, in a polite way.) Guests who come to our church and don't see genuine love and care from us will quickly reject our church. How sad it is that the majority of employees at *Chic-fli-A* are more courteous and helpful than folks in church.

III. Evangelism's models – The Christian life

I have a friend whom I have admired for over thirty years. He is a professor at a major university, holds a doctor of philosophy degree; and is a leader in his scientific field. He is kind, loving, and lives a simple lifestyle. He is faithful to his wife and family. The church has always been an integral part of his life. He serves as a teacher, is a small group leader, and is active in other ministries. He is generous and has a missionary heart. What impressed me over the years was his unassuming nature. I would best describe him as a person of humility. Even though we have traveled in different circles for the past decade, I think of him, pray for him and always enjoy the times when we reconnect.

Following Christ, going for Christ, and sharing the gospel are integral parts of a daily lifetime ministry. When a Christian awakens to a new day, he should be praying for sensitivity of the Holy Spirit's leadership during the day. Whoever crosses his path would see Jesus in him. In our busyness, hurriedness, and agenda-driven lives, we quench the Spirit's activity in our daily lives. Thus, many honk their car horns, are rude to the restaurant waiters, and are harsh towards their fellow workers for their own cause and not for Christ. How can one invite someone to his church when one acts in such a manner? How can one have "Jesus is the Way" on a bumper sticker and be a bully driver. Christ set the example, the Apostles wrote about it, and they set the standard on how to relate to others. If the Christian cannot be in life ministry daily, I believe he becomes a hypocrite (play actor) when he undertakes a ministry in the church.

A few men wanted a certain individual to serve on a ministry team in a church I served. The man they desired was cocky, self absorbed, shallow spiritually, but knowledgeable in his field. which would benefit the church. I stiff armed their recommendation and I would not allow their suggested individual to serve. Again, if the fruit of the Spirit is not sweet, then the person does need not be in ministry, and, maybe, he needs to evaluate his relationship.

IV. The Christian's ministry – Use spiritual gifts.

Every Christian has a spiritual gift(s) given by the Holy Spirit for the good of the Body of Christ (I Corinthians 12:7, 11). There are numerous spiritual gift inventories from which to choose, and I suggest that passion for a certain ministry be the key to unlocking a person's giftedness. Sometimes the passion is discovered through trial and error. One may teach children only to find how laborious and joyless it becomes. On the other hand, working with the homeless community may provide energy, joy, and a wealth of ideas of how better to minister to this group of folk. In other words, one ministry is dreaded; the other is invigorating.

I read years ago of a man in his eighties who was still ministering to the youth in his church. The youth loved him, and he obviously loved them. God ordained ministry before the foundation of the world for His children to undertake (Ephesians 2:10). Then God, the Holy Spirit, manifests the gift in the believer's life. As one continues in the ministry calling of God's choosing, the child of God sees fruit and senses fulfillment in life.

A church driven by committees does an injustice to the majority of the congregation. Many churches promote committee involvement more than ministry participation. The church I mentioned earlier had forty-two committees.

The emphasis was on filling the required number for each committee. The nominating committee had the responsibility of finding people to fill these positions. Many times a warm body, not an eager one, was found to fill a vacancy, and the person became frustrated after a period of time and stopped attending the meetings. If a church of two thousand has forty-two committees, each needing approximately five persons, only two hundred ten people serve. What about the other eighteen hundred members? Churches need to promote ministry more than committee involvement. Ministry meets the needs of others in the love of Jesus.

V. The Christian's mission – Reach people.

Missions is related to the community where the church is located and beyond it boundaries. Ministry involves reaching people in the church and in the church's community. Missions as ministry is demonstrating the love of Jesus and sharing how one can have a relationship with Him. Missions is not social ministry, although it has social aspects. Many churches have a fourfold ministry/mission strategy: Church and Local (ministries) and National and Global (missions). To fulfill their mission endeavors churches either create a mission or link with an existing mission.

For example, my brother, Rick, founded MissionLink, International. Some from my churches have supported the mission financially, and others have participated by going to Uganda with him regularly. Still others have served through the International Mission Board of the Southern Baptist Convention, either vocationally or short-term. The reality is that there are numerous missions with which individuals can link arms to further the kingdom of God. In doing so, they will be more fulfilled and fruitful in their walk with the Lord. As importantly, the watching eyes of those peering into our churches will see a people more concerned for others than themselves.

Evangelism is the key component in demonstrating an authentic life to the watching community. The outsider wants to know whether the church cares for others and for him. In other words, our words have to have heart and feet. This is why in Paul's letters he gives doctrine but concludes with application. One could hear James' mandate through his pointed statement, "Faith without works is useless" (2:20). Wow! Does this scripture drive you from your easy chair to serve in the kingdom of God? This verse is like someone throwing cold water on your face. You wake up to the real Christian life. You've heard the saying, "If you only sit in the pew you will stew." Have you ever let food expire? An unpleasant aroma surrounds it, and it is inedible. As James said, it is useless. Enough said!

Ministry and missions are the vehicles of evangelism that will keep us fresh and useful. The focus of the church will be reaching people, not managing the church. Jesus said it simply but with heart, "GO!" As you go through life, acknowledge Jesus so that He will acknowledge you before the Father (Matthew 10:32).

VI. Evangelism's Major Warning – Expect Persecution!

In Matthew 10:24 Jesus clearly states that a slave is not above his master. When Jesus sat and taught what we call the Sermon on the Mount, he clearly spoke that whoever follows Him will be persecuted (Matthew 5:10). Paul addresses persecution throughout his letters, and James teaches that we should count it all joy when you face various trials. Persecution is one of those tribulations. One of the themes of Peter's first letter highlights the suffering of the Christian. One of my first teachers prior to my call to preach was Dick Woodward. His conclusion of Jesus' sermon: when you take the character of the beatitudes into your culture, you will create a crisis. Paul wrote young Timothy to tell him, "…to suffer hardship with him as a good soldier of Christ" (II Timothy 2:3). Plus, all who desire to live a godly life in Christ Jesus will be persecuted (II Timothy 3:12). Persecution is the badge a Christian wears telling of his faithfulness to Jesus. It identifies the believer as a resident in the kingdom of God. It shows his high position on earth as an ambassador of his King Jesus, reconciling others to move into His kingdom (II Corinthians 5:20).

Another glance at Grace Mountain:

LIVING CHIRST'S CHARACTER IN
CULTURE CREATES A CRISIS

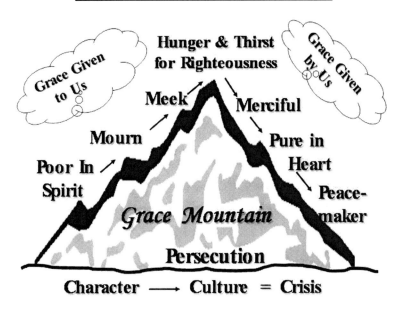

Looking again at the above diagram from a slightly different perspective, the Christian's bankrupt spirit mourns his sin and the sins of others. He realizes the grace received from the Lord, creating an attitude of humility (not thinking too highly of one's self) which leads him to hunger and to thirst for Jesus' righteousness and to live under God's umbrella of grace. When the follower of Jesus descends Grace Mountain into his culture, he involuntary displays Jesus. He is merciful towards others, his life has a single focus which is the Lord, and he is a peacemaker.

He understands that the world is totally opposite in attitude and behavior. The world is self-focused, only hungering and thirsting after its heart's treasure. As Jesus taught, "for where your treasure is, there your heart will be also" (Matthew 6:21). Realize that taking a Jesus-centered life into a man- centered world, will create a crisis. Don't be surprised! Persecution will come! Endure! Endure family rejections, a friend's negativity, and workplace frustrations. Allow the Holy Spirit to lead and to provide the words needed for the situation.

Now a word to the pastor or transitional pastor or elder: don't be surprised by the rejection you may receive when you teach and display God's righteousness and grace to your congregation. As shared earlier, you are dealing with non-believers, immature believers, and mature believers. Many will not like having their lives challenged. Endure! Remember, Christ suffered. We are not above our Master.

The leaders of the church must handle light persecution to teach the saints to handle the persecution that is becoming greater in our own country.

Conclusion

Yes, a Christian without a missionary heart is abnormal. Evangelism is the "Go" in the Great Commission to make disciples. These disciples then multiply the kingdom of God, making America and the world a more beautiful place to live for His glory. I pray that every Jesus centered church will pray as Paul:

" Praying at the same time for us as well, that God will open up to us a door for the word, so that we may speak forth the mystery of Christ, for which I have also been imprisoned" (Colossians 4:3).

Pray as Jesus instructed; "Jesus *said to them, "My food is to do the will of Him who sent Me and to accomplish His work. [35] Do you not say, 'There are yet four months, and *then* comes the harvest'? Behold, I say to you, lift up your eyes and look on the fields, that they are white for harvest" (John 4:34-35).

Or Matthew 9:36-37 reads: "Seeing the people, He felt compassion for them, because they were distressed and dispirited like sheep without a shepherd. [37] Then He *said to His disciples, "The harvest is plentiful, but the workers are few."

Jesus taught the church to open her eyes to see people not problems. He promised that there would be a harvest. Second, Jesus told us to pray for laborers to go into the fields to reap the harvest. People will have their hearts regenerated, their sin recognized, and repentance realized, for their sins will be forgiven. Righteousness has been credited to them by the grace of God. Around each church there are people who are ready to be harvested. Will your church send out the necessary laborers to bring them into the kingdom of God? Or reader, will you go?

R.E.S.C.U.E.

A Final Word of Encouragement

You have read stories of pastors and staff who suffered, because their church hit a church iceberg. I have been honest with my failures and successes over my thirty year ministry. Unfortunately, some of the stories of each chapter ended dramatically: pastors forced to resign, pastors experiencing moral failures, or pastors exhausted by the church bully. I want to encourage you, pastor, to persevere in the heat of your battle. Evaluate what has to change in your life. If necessary, apologize, ask for forgiveness, and try to reconcile with those not in your corner. Pray for those who persecute you, and love your enemies. Open the curtain of your heart to show the grace on your heart's stage. Moses told the people of Israel as they stood before the Red Sea and with an army of Egyptian warriors behind them; [13] "But Moses said to the people, "Do not fear! Stand by and see the salvation of the LORD which He will accomplish for you today; for the Egyptians whom you have seen today, you will never see them again forever. [14] The LORD will fight for you while you keep silent." (Exodus 14:13-14). Moses stated five truths for the church today:

1. Fear not,
2. Stand firm,

3. Watch God work for you today,
4. Watch God fight for you, and
5. Be silent.

My prayer is that you not fear the sea of church icebergs, that the church be able to stand firm and see the mighty hand of the Lord restore it; and that that God will bring to fruition a restored church to be used as His instrument for His glory.

Finally, folks in the pew, listen. If you are the church bully or power broker, humble yourself under the mighty hand of God. He is not pleased with your behavior, and you do not honor His church. Reconcile with a fellow parishioner, staff person, or family member. You are not there to run the church. You are a minister to meet someone's need in the love of Jesus. Stop being a troublemaker and become a peacemaker. Not peacekeeper but maker. Keepers traditionally tolerate or close their eyes to the reality of other's behavior. Peacemakers encourage others to change their behavior. Be a unity maker for your church. If you cannot do this, maybe you have to evaluate your salvation. What is your relationship with the Lord? Is having your way more important than having unity in your church? Let me encourage you not to be an iceberg with which your church collides. Live Exodus 14:13-14!

One of the most beautiful wonders on the planet is a church that is walking together in love, in the light of Christ, and with Biblical wisdom. Restored relationships, courageous evaluation of the church's reality, expectations of staff and congregation applied, streamlined governance that frees the people to minister, and a concise and clear vision and mission as the church's compass, will create a unified evangelistic body of believers. R.E.S.C.U.E. will keep your ship, your church fellowship afloat! Lord Jesus, let it be!

CPSIA information can be obtained at www.ICGtesting.com
Printed in the USA
BVOW07s0052271014

372341BV00001B/13/P